OVERCOMING GIANTS

Overcoming Giants
Copyright @ 2021 by Abraham 'Wole Haastrup

All rights reserved. No part of this book may be produced, stored in a retrieval system, or transmitted in any form or by any means–electronic, mechanical, photocopy, recording, scanning, or any other – except for brief quotations in printed reviews, without the permission of the publisher.

Global Kingdom Influence (GKI)
(Biblical Truth, Leadership, & Christian Advocacy)

Coburg North, Vic 3059, Australia.

ISBN 978–0–9923823-6-0

Unless otherwise indicated, Scripture quotations are from The New King James Version of the Holy Bible, copyright 1982 – Thomas Nelson, Inc. used by permission.

Printed in Nigeria - **House of Israel Publishing Company**
Plot 3, Block 4, Estate 12, RCCG. Redemption Camp, Ogun State, Nigeria.
Plot3, Omoniyi Estate, Off Benin/Owo Expressway, Akure, Ondo State, Nigeria. Tel: +234-8034082781, +234-8096588871.
e-mail: houseofisreal2020@gmail.com

Other Books by the same author:

- God Still Speaks Today

- High Praise

- Obedience - The Secret of Miracles

- In Remembrance of Me

- Your Last Hope

- The Secret of Divine Favour

- Ebenezer (God Can Do It Again)

- The Christian Worker

- Nations At Rage

- The Almighty Formulae

- The First Voice

- The Third Epistle (A Leadership Reminiscence)

TABLE OF CONTENTS

Preface		v
Introduction		vii
1.	**God's Masterpiece**	**10**
1.1	God's masterpiece	11
1.2	Divinely Empowered	19
1.3	Head, Not Tail	31
1.4	Unstoppable Glory	43
2.	**Overcoming Giants**	**58**
2.1	Overcoming Giants	59
2.2	Don't Give Up!	73
2.3	In Tune With God	85
2.4	A Stop-Over in Haran	99
2.5	Enough is Enough	107
2.6	Oh Lord, Remember Me!	119
3.	**The God of all possibilities**	**134**
3.1	The God of all possibilities	135
3.2	The Unchangeable Changer	151
3.3	Who is Like unto Thee, O Lord?	159
3.4	Let the Fire Fall!	167
3.5	A Miracle like a Dream	175
Acknowledgments		192

Preface

The basic ingredients for the content of this book- "Overcoming Giants", came from the various sermons, techings, and ministry opportunities which God gave us as part of our assignments as a Missionary in the Australia/Pacific Region of the Redeemed Christian Church of God. In preparing to preach or teach the topics covered, God used the periods to speak to me as a person. I am very grateful to God for His love and mercy. As Apostle Paul wrote in Col 9:27, I continue to pray for myself too that I will not be found guilty of doing what I asked others not to do. Equally, that I will not be found guilty of not doing what I asked others to do.

May all that God will make known to you through this book make you a better child of God. May your light continue to shine, may you remain an example of a totally true Christian, even in these last days in Jesus Name.

Introduction

In addition to (and in place of) the good seed which God sowed into man at creation, Satan, in the Garden of Eden introduced a new nature of sin - with all its attendant evils and woes. Thus, it can be said that every man has two potentials - two Giants - positive and negative, constructive and destructive. The fallen man also loved many things that had the tendency to make or mar his personal destiny.

In this book "*Overcoming Giants*", God will open your eyes to recognize your two sides - your positive and negative Giants. You will also discover some tools that you can use in overcoming the negative giants in and around you - be they internal or external Giants, or even human, spiritual, and institutional Giants. The author looked at some Biblical personalities who though were great, but failed to overcome some Giants in their lives. Finally, the need to watch over some Gates in our lives so they will not become ready doors for Satan to pass through was emphasized.

In our earlier book *"The Almighty Formulae"*, the issue of Gates was extensively discussed. Some things to do to ensure constant victories at our gates were also pointed out. Now, in relation to Giants, there is need to pay attention to what passes through the vital Gates of our lives, as these can make or mar a man's glorious destiny. The story continued to be told of the Great Wall of China. Not only was it thick and imposing, its strong Gates were manned 24/7. In spite of all these, however, the enemies still penetrated through it. Why? - All because the men on duty lacked integrity and patriotism. Bought over by the external forces, they let down their guards!

If we too will be victorious daily, and ultimately at the end of our race on earth, we must ask God to help us defeat every giant at the following gates of our lives:
* our eyes - what do we look at? (Job 31:1; II Sam 11:1-6, 14-17)
* our ears - who and what do we listen to? (Psalm 1:1)
* our minds - what thoughts fill us up or occupy us? (Proverbs 32:7).

* our hands - what do we touch, take or even write? (II Sam 11:14-17; Esther 3:6; Acts 28:8)
* our feet - where do they carry us to? (Psalm 37:23, 31).
* our mouth - what goes in and out of our mouth? (Luke 6:45).
* or, tongue - What do we say with our tongue (Does your tongue need healing?) (James 3:2).

In addition to the central theme of 'Overcoming Giants', this book also discusses other subjects, each of which in itself should help the spiritual growth of the reader. As you go through the book, may you have a life-changing encounter in Jesus Name, Amen. Happy reading.

GOD'S MASTERPIECE

1.1 God's masterpiece

1.2 Divinely Empowered

1.3 Head, Not Tail

1.4 Unstoppable Glory

God's Masterpiece

"8 God saved you by His grace when you believed. And you can't take credit for this; it is a gift from God. 9 Salvation is not a reward for the good things we have done, so none of us can boast about it. 10 For we are God's masterpiece. He has created us anew in Christ Jesus, so we can do the good things He planned for us long ago. 11 Don't forget that you Gentiles used to be outsiders. You were called "uncircumcised heathens" by the Jews, who were proud of their circumcision, even though it affected only their bodies and not their hearts. 12 In those days you were living apart from Christ. You were excluded from citizenship among the people of Israel, and you did

not know the covenant promises God had made to them. You lived in this world without God and without hope. 13 But now you have been united with Christ Jesus. Once you were far away from God, but now you have been brought near to him through the blood of Christ."

(Ephesians 2:8-10 NLT)

Our focus will be Vs 10:
"For we are God's masterpiece. He has created us anew in Christ Jesus, so we can do the good things He planned for us long ago."

Even though there is a lot to see even in this Verse, we will narrow our discussion to the word "Masterpiece"

The word 'Masterpiece' refers, among others, to:
-   a great work, something done with an extraordinary skill. It is also said to be "a piece of work presented as evidence for qualification for the rank of a MASTER!

Looked at more closely, one will also note that the word 'Masterpiece' is a compound word made up of 'Master' and 'piece'

- From these definitions, some things also become clear about God:
- He is God- He alone is God and He is God alone! Isaiah 40:18, 25 says:

   "To whom then will you liken God? Or what likeness will you compare to Him?. "To whom then will you liken Me, Or to whom shall I be equal?" says the Holy One. Lift up your eyes on high, And see who has created these things, Who brings out their host by number;"

- He is a Master. In fact, He is the Master - He is Master <u>at all</u> and the Master <u>of all</u>, and Master over all –all Creation and all the created - both visible and invisible (Colossians 1:13-20). He is preeminent, He is superior to all principalities and powers.

At creation, the Bible said God dropped a little piece of Himself into man, and man became a living soul. That made each one of us a Masterpiece.

However, that undying nature and presence of God in man made us a target of the devil. The devil succeeded in stealing that piece from Adam. When this happened, a vital piece became missing. Now, when a vital piece is missing in a whole, the rest will be in pieces! The main reason Jesus came to die in our place is to restore what the enemy stole.

That is why until every piece yield to Him, they can not be fulfilled. Neither will they be able to fulfil their purpose in life (John 15:1-5).
Not Only is God Master in all the things He has created including we human beings, He is also Master at putting <u>pieces</u> together.

May be you are reading this book, and your life is in a mess - everything seem to be in pieces. Jesus is a specialist at putting pieces back together. Before this day is over, may God intervene in your case in Jesus mighty Name. May God give a meaningful whole to your life. May He give you a brand new beginning in Jesus Name (II Corinthians 5:17). Has God done such a thing before? The answer is YES! In John 4:1-end, Jesus met a woman whose life was in pieces. Before that day ended, she experienced a new beginning.

Perhaps yours is a life that seem to be full of misfortunes, and you cannot understand why everything seem not to be going smoothly. Joseph may have thought so too. His life started with dreams of greatness, but all unfolding events seemed to prove otherwise. In spite of all these, Joseph stood with God, and God too showed up for Him (Genesis 37:5-9; Genesis 39:7-9; Genesis 41:14-45; Genesis 45:1-8; Genesis 50:19-20).

Now, one of the evils of sin was that the original piece which God deposited in man was contaminated. That initial piece could no longer fulfil God's purpose and agenda.

At Salvation, we come to be restored to our original place with God - we are cleansed and restored to God's plan and purpose. We can now begin to do the things God created us to do at the beginning (Vs 10 NLT).

Once again, dear reader, may I assure you that you are not an accident of nature. God has a great plan for you. No matter where you are and what you may be going through, don't abandon God, He will fulfil His plan for your life - You are God's Masterpiece! If you are already genuinely saved, know that God saved you so that you could become what He had in mind - a very long time ago.

What must you do if this will happen?
Cooperate with God – the truth is, without Him, you cannot succeed. God created you for a great purpose. Without Him you cannot realize that purpose, let alone fulfil it. But with Him,

nothing can stop you! And, if there is anything or anyone that appears to be stopping you, very soon, He or she will become history! Mrs Potiphar became history. The Brothers of Joseph who sold him to slavery ended up bowing before him. What of the Pharaoh who said the Israelites will not be free to go and serve God? God drowned him, and he too became history!

If up to now you have refused to accept Jesus into your life, you are doing so to the detriment of your destiny. Please stop it, and accept Him as your Saviour, Lord and King, today. Wherever your are even right now, you need to repent of your sins. You need to confess those sins to God (you can get a Bible and open to these Scriptures: Isaiah 55:6-6; Acts 4:12; I John 1:5-9; Proverbs 28:13. Please pray this prayer:

"Lord Jesus, I have personally sinned against You in my thoughts, in my words and in my actions. There is nothing I can do on my own to take away my sin. I deserve to go to hell, but You died for a helpless sinner like me so I can be forgiven. I surrender myself to You completely. Please take away all my sins and come into my heart by Your Holy Spirit, and be my own Saviour and Lord, and do with me as You desire. Help me to follow You at all cost. Thank You for hearing my prayer, and for coming into my heart, Amen."

Our Text (Ephesians 2:10) said Jesus saved us and made us a Masterpiece so we can fulfil what God had in mind a long time ago. As a masterpiece, we are carriers of His nature, character, power, and authority (I John 1:4-7; John 8:12; Matthew 5: 13-16; Luke 10:19). It means anywhere we are, we carry and should manifest who our Father is.

It has often been said that ignorance of the purpose of something can lead to abuse. If you don't know who you are and whose you are, the world is waiting to redefine you.

Satan too is there to give you his own definition of who he wants you to be!

This also leads us to the fact that even though God is a divine Sculptor, yet He needs you to cooperate with Him so that His original plan can come to pass in your life. It is your obedience that makes this possible. If on the other hand, through your continual disobedience you provoke Him to abandon you, or you wound yourself and render yourself unusable, you will regret at the end.

Divinely Empowered

"Fear not, for I am with you; Be not dismayed, for I am your God. I will strengthen you, Yes, I will help you, I will uphold you with My righteous right hand.' "Behold, all those who were incensed against you Shall be ashamed and disgraced; They shall be as nothing, And those who strive with you shall perish. You shall seek them and not find them—Those who contended with you. Those who war against you Shall be as nothing, As a nonexistent thing. For I, the Lord your God, will hold your right hand, Saying to you, 'Fear not, I will help you.'"

(Isaiah 41:10-13)

I don't know if you have ever heard God's voice, or even believe that there is a God who speaks. May I tell you that the One who is speaking here is the Almighty God Himself. He is speaking to you in particular, as a person. His word is to you, and for you. His word to you here is: "I will 'SHU' you", that is, God will strengthen you; He will help you, and God will uphold you. God went on here to group your enemies into four categories, and declared what will befall everyone of them. Receive your permanent victory in Jesus Name.

Among many things, in this Chapter, we shall be discussing:
- What it means to be Divinely Empowered,
- Why we do need to be positively and divinely empowered,
- What a person becomes and does when he/she is Divinely Empowered
- How God does empower His people,
- A few examples of people who were Divinely Empowered.

Power is a very critical subject, this is because of it's importance. Power is said to be the ability to do something.

Power can be looked at from different perspectives– for example, in terms of it's sources, it's nature, and what it can do or make people do:
Just for the purpose of illustration, if I request you to rise up; turn to your right side; and I then ask you to shout Hallelujah. What have I just done? - I have exercised a form of power towards you right where you are, and all the way from where I am!

In terms of its <u>nature</u>, power can be physical or spiritual.

Physical power can include - mental, financial, political, economic power, etc. It also includes the physical strength to carry heavy loads.

Spiritual power can include: anointing, supernatural strength, the operation of the gifts of the Holy Spirit, etc.

I once knew a young man (he is a one-man 'music house'. When he is on the Keyboard, it will sound as if a whole orchestra is playing.

Supernatural power refers to the kind of power that is more than natural, or is beyond men. Another word for supernatural power is divine power.

Supernatural or divine power can be positive or negative. That is, it can be godly or ungodly. It will be noted that the word 'divination' is a derivative of the word 'divine'. The Bible in several places warned against divination (Deuteronomy 18:10-14; II Kings 17:17-18). In particular, Acts 16:16-24 referred to a young lady who used a spirit of divination (also called a Python spirit).

Operating or ministering under the influence of the spirit of divination can be so subtle and deceptive that it may take some time before even great men of God (like Apostle Paul) could discern it!

Today, there are many "gospel" Artists that one can easily say that the spirit behind their songs is of God, but when you look beyond the surface, this may not really be so.

By God's grace, we shall be devoting the rest of this chapter to the positive side of the word 'Divine'.

To be powered or empowered means to be given some assistance that makes the person (so empowered), to be an outstanding performer or achiever - either positively or negatively. People like Samson, David, Solomon, Prophets Elijah & Elisha, Daniel, etc, were positively empowered.

On the other hand, the magicians of Pharaoh, and the woman called Jezebel, etc were negatively empowered. Also, our Lord Jesus and His Disciples (especially Peter and Paul), and others were positively empowered.

To be positively and supernaturally or divinely empowered is very important, if not critical for us as Christians, and as people who are living in a time like this. Today, may God divinely empower you in Jesus Name.

Why do we need to be positively and divinely empowered?

First, we need it so we can discern people, situations and events around us. In these end times, there are lots of deception and manipulation, both within and outside the Church. We need to be divinely empowered so we don't become deceived and manipulated. Many "Thus says the Lord", or "the Lord is leading me to ask you to...", may not be totally from God!

Second, we need to be divinely empowered so we can live a victorious life. The battles and challenges of daily living demand that we be divinely empowered (please go and read Psalm 91:1-10; II Corinthians 10:3-6; Ephesians 6:10-18; II Corinthians 2:11).

Third, we need it so we can fulfil our destiny and God's purpose. Part of the realities and challenges of life (whether we believe it or not), is that enemies of destiny abound. They are not just out to hinder or slow you down, they are outright destiny destroyers! The stories of Joseph, David, and even our Lord Jesus show us very clearly that there are destiny destroyers (see Genesis 37:5-11, 13-20; Genesis 39:7-12; I Samuel 18:6-10, 21, 25; Matthew 2:1-5, 7, 12-16). Divine empowerment will always ensure that in the end, we fulfil God's purpose (see also Psalm 89:22-24).

Finally, we need divine empowerment so we can be a channel of blessing. Salvation, healing and deliverance of people and nations are made possible when we are divinely empowered.

I had an experience not too long ago- I was at a city square (a very central train and bus terminal) to share Gospel leaflets (Tracts). An acrobat cum enchanter was also on stand. He started to bewitch the crowd, and no one was willing to listen to us. So, I found a small corner of the Square, and began to pray. Within five minutes, the sky suddenly became dark and rain began to fall. Everyone dispersed. The few that took refuge where I was gladly received the word of Life. Our God is awesome! May HE divinely empower you today in Jesus Name.

There is an assignment God has given to us as His children and followers; we are commanded to establish God's Kingdom here on Earth (Matthew 6: 6-10). We are also to make Disciples of all nations (Mark 16:15-18; Acts 1:8).

In Matthew 5:13-16, our Lord Jesus reminded us about who we really are –the salt of the earth, and the light of the world. He commanded us to penetrate and positively influence our world - beginning from our immediate environment.

Furthermore, in Romans 4:13, we find something many of us may not have been paying particular attention to. This is the fact that sometimes ago, God gave what we can describe as the certificate of occupancy (the C of O) of the entire world to one man –the man ABRAHAM –(Vs 17-25).

All who are truly and genuinely Born Again are the seed of Abraham - the spiritual Israel (Galatians 3:13-18). Now, there is no true child who would see the property of his father (and in essence, his own inheritance, being desecrated or wasted and vandalized or being devalued, and would keep quiet, fold his hands, or turn his or her eyes in the opposite direction. We therefore have the moral and spiritual duty to forbid further advancements of the Adversary. It is also our urgent responsibility to recover all the adversary had illegally taken over – both human and material. To me, I think this is the whole essence of being the salt and the light.

At Creation, God divinely empowered the human race (Genesis 1:26-28). When sin came, that authority was lost. However, and even before Jesus Christ came physically into the world, God directly intervened and divinely empowered a few people as needed. Let us look at a few examples of people who were divinely empowered, and how they affected their generations. Such men included Abraham and Jacob (Genesis 12:1-5; Genesis 17:1-16; Genesis 28:10-18), Moses and Joshua(Exodus 3:1-7; Deuteronomy 34:9-14; Joshua1:1-5), David (I Samuel 16:7-13: Elijah and Elisha (I Kings 18:21-38); II Kings 1:10-15; II Kings 2:9-15),Paul the Apostle (Acts 9:1-9),etc.

Of course, God also divinely empowered the Lord Jesus too Matthew 3:14-17. In particular, Acts 10:38 declares:
> ***"How God anointed Jesus of Nazareth with the Holy Spirit and with power, who went about doing good and healing all who were oppressed by the devil, for God was with Him."***

When Christ resurrected, the opportunity for every true child of God to be divinely empowered became available. In Matthew 28:18-20, the resurrected and victorious Jesus declared:

> "*And Jesus came and spoke to them, saying,* "*All authority has been given to Me in heaven and on earth.* ¹⁹*Go therefore and make disciples of all the nations, baptizing them in the name of the Father and of the Son and of the Holy Spirit,* ²⁰*teaching them to observe all things that I have commanded you; and lo, I am with you always, even to the end of the age.*" *Amen.*"
>
> **(See also Acts 1:8, Acts 19:11-12).**

In the Book of Acts, we see divinely empowered people at work for God. In contemporary times as well as today, all across the world, God has His vessels whom He had equipped.
By God's grace, the General Overseer of the RCCG – a dear father-in-the-Lord, is a man divinely empowered by God for His end-time agenda.

How does God empower His people? He does so in various ways. He could, through His word or by the Holy Spirit. God can also empower through the outpouring of His anointing upon them. In some cases, God can do so by declaration and pronouncement of a spiritual leader as He did for Joshua through Moses (Deuteronomy 34:9), David through Samuel (I Samuel 16:7-13), Elisha through Elijah (I Kings 19:19-21), and the young Timothy through the Presbytery as well as Apostle Paul (I Timothy 4:13-16; II Timothy 1:6-7).

God can also directly reach a man in a dream or vision and empower him. That was what He did to or with Abraham, Jacob, Joshua, Solomon, etc.

God is not unaware of the fact that power could be a dangerous thing when it is in the hands of an enemy. Hence, He will not empower just any Dick or Harry.

To be divinely empowered, there are a few steps to take:
The starting point is a genuine repentance which brings Salvation. Salvation brings a person into a personal relationship with God and makes him a candidate for divine empowerment. Even as you are reading this book, if you will settle the issue of your relationship with God, He can empower you. In addition to being a true child of God, if you can assure God that you will use the power only for His glory, then, He will be more than willing to deposit His power in your life.

It's time to pray:
- Father, thank You for Your word, thank You for opening my eyes. Please increase my faith in You.
- Father, I need Your power, please divinely empower me.

- Father, I need Your power to fulfil my purpose and destiny, today and right now, send your power to me (Acts 1:8; Acts 10:38).

You can check out the lyrics of this song/Hymn: "*Holy Spirit come.....*
Send Your power to us from on High x3...
Come Holy Spirit come"

Finally, please go back to the opening scriptures at the beginning of this chapter, and confidently personalize the promises:
+ fear not, I am with you" – I shall not fear, God is with me.
+ I shall not be dismayed (confused), the Almighty is my God.
+ God will strengthen me, He will help me, He will uphold me with His right hand of righteousness.
+ All those who were incensed against me SHALL be ashamed and disgraced,
+ Those who strive with me SHALL perish!
+ Those who contend with me and those who war against me SHALL be as nothing - as next to nothing!
+ The Lord my God will hold my right hand. and while He is still holding my right hand, I will continue to hear His re-assuring voice saying: "FEAR NOT, I WILL HELP YOU"!

Head, Not Tail

"Now it shall come to pass, if you diligently obey the voice of the Lord your God, to observe carefully all His commandments which I command you today, that the Lord your God will set you high above all nations of the earth. And all these blessings shall come upon you and overtake you, because you obey the voice of the Lord your God:...And the Lord will make you the head and not the tail; you shall be above only, and not be beneath, if you heed the commandments of the Lord your God, which I command you today, and are careful to observe them. So you shall not turn aside from any of the words **which I command you this day, to the right or the**

left, to go after other gods to serve them."
(Deuteronomy 28:1-2, 13-4).

"HEAD NOT TAIL" say it after me: "HEAD NOT TAIL". Now declare: I Will be a HEAD, and NOT a TAIL"!

'Head !' What does it mean or stand for? The head is the upper or anterior part or division of the animal body. It contains the brain, the chief sense organs, and the mouth. The head is also the seat of the intellect - a person's mental ability - the mind or intellect. The 'head' can refer to a person with respect to mental qualities.

What about the word 'Tail?' It is said to be the rear end or prolongation of the rear end of the body of an animal. 'Tail' also refers to the back, the last, the lower, or the inferior part of something.

Can you rise up and shout again: "I WILL BE HEAD AND NOT TAIL!"

Among others, there are five peculiarities of the Head that are worth noting:
* Everything God made has a head - whether man, animals, birds, fishes, etc. In the same manner and following God's

pattern, everything that man has devised or manufactured, has a head.

* The head is always on top or in front. This should straight away tell us some things very special about the head: It is designed to be above, to carry responsibility, or to be in front - to lead and give direction!
* The head always have some special organs and features: in the Head we have the brain, the eyes, the ears, the nose and the mouth. Of course the mouth itself is made up of the lips, the tongue, the teeth, etc).
* Each of the organs or features in the Head is meant for specific functions and roles. For example, the brain, the eyes, the ears, the nose, the mouth (including the lips, the tongue, and teeth).
* The master plan of God for me and you is to be the Head and never the tail. He also made it clear in His Word (the Holy Bible), what we need to do to be head and not become a tail. By His decision to make us a Head, God was and is still aiming at something –DOMINION!

As we hinted earlier, to be a Head means being on top or up on a ladder and hierarchy. It has been observed that often, some people aspire to be the head, or to lead for different reasons.

Some people want to be head for glamour rather than to take responsibilities. Some want to be head to exercise authority or to lord it over people rather than to serve. Some even want to be on top so as to amass wealth.

It should be noted that becoming head is a huge responsibility. It is to be a blessing, and a change agent. It is to see ahead. Very importantly, becoming a head involves some processes.

Before Abraham became great, and also the father of Nations as God promised him, a lot happened to him. Before Joseph ended up in the palace as Prime Minister in Egypt, he experienced the pit, the prison, and loneliness. He landed in prison not because he did anything wrong, but for doing what was right! The good thing is that the God whom Joseph feared, and would not sin against, showed up for him. If you too will fear God and not sin against him, no matter what men try to do to you, the same God will show up for you in Jesus Name.

Before David ascended the throne as king over Israel and Judah, he faced many adversaries - both at home and abroad.

Before our Lord Jesus got a Name that is above all names, Philippians 2:5-8 tell us:

"Let this mind be in you which was also in Christ Jesus, who, being in the form of God, did not consider it robbery to be equal with God, but made Himself of no reputation, taking the form of a bond servant, and coming in the likeness of men. And being found in appearance as a man, He humbled Himself and became obedient to the point of death, even the death of the cross. Therefore God also has highly exalted Him and given Him the name which is above every name, that at the name of Jesus every knee should bow, of those in heaven, and of those on earth, and of those under the earth, and that every tongue should confess that Jesus Christ is Lord, to the glory of God the Father."

To the glory of God, before God made the General Overseer of RCCG what the whole world came to know him to be today - a voice for God in this our generation, - he too went through a process.

What are the things to do, or the conditions to fulfill, if we will be who and what God wants us to be - a Head, and not a tail?

Let us look at our Text (Deuteronomy 28:13-14) again:
> *"And the Lord will make you the head and not the tail; you shall be above only, and not be beneath, if you heed the commandments of the Lord your God, which I command you today, and are careful to observe them. So you shall not turn aside from any of the words which I command you this day, to the right or the left, to go after other gods to serve them."*

In the NLT, the same passage reads thus:
> *"If you listen to these commands of the lord your God that I am giving you today, and if you carefully obey them, the lord will make you the head and not the tail, and you will always be on top and never at the bottom. You must not turn away from any of the commands I am giving you today, nor follow after other gods and worship them."*

Note what this passage says: it is the Lord who will make you and me head, and not the Tail. How will God do it? I don't know too. One thing I know is that He can do it anyhow - PROVIDED WE WILL LET HIM DO IT! How can we let Him? God will do it if;

*   we heed His word;
*   we are careful to observe them;

* we do not turn aside from any of His words;
* we don't go after other gods to serve them.

In practical terms, what do all these mean?
1.   To heed His Word means we do it. This will rarely happen if we don't first study the Bible to know who God is, and what He has said in His Word – the Holy Bible. A man cannot do what he does not know about, or understand. When we talk about understanding here, we are not saying that God will tell you the reasons for what He is asking you to do. In most cases He will not. But you know for sure, what He is saying to you. Several years ago, I wanted to stay in UK, God said DON'T! Rather, He said 'go to East Africa as a Missionary'. That was well over 30 Years ago. Up till now, He has not told me the reasons. However, looking back, I have no single regret! I give God all the glory.

2.   To heed God's Word also means not going after other gods - that was the problem of king Solomon. In I Kings 11:1-2, 4-6, 9-11, we read:

> *"But King Solomon loved many foreign women, as well as the daughter of Pharaoh: women of the Moabites, Ammonites, Edomites, Sidonians, and Hittites— ² from the nations of whom the* LORD *had said to the children of Israel, "You shall not intermarry with them, nor they with you. Surely they*

will turn away your hearts after their gods." Solomon clung to these in love... For it was so, when Solomon was old, that his wives turned his heart after other gods; and his heart was not loyal to the LORD his God, as was the heart of his father David. For Solomon went after Ashtoreth the goddess of the Sidonians, and after Milcom the abomination of the Ammonites. ⁶Solomon did evil in the sight of the LORD, and did not fully follow the LORD, as did his father David... So the LORD became angry with Solomon, because his heart had turned from the LORD God of Israel, who had appeared to him twice, ¹⁰ and had commanded him concerning this thing, that he should not go after other gods; but he did not keep what the LORD had commanded. ¹¹ Therefore the LORD said to Solomon, "Because you have done this, and have not kept My covenant and My statutes, which I have commanded you, I will surely tear the kingdom away from you and give it to your servant."

(See also I Corinthians 11:1-3; John 15:1-5; Hebrews 1:9; Hebrews 12:2; Hebrews 12:14).

Also, and very crucial, if we will be head and not tail, we must not be ignorant. Hosea 4:6, says:

> *"My people are destroyed for lack of knowledge. Because you have rejected knowledge, I also will reject you from being priest for Me; Because you have forgotten the law of your God, I also will forget your children."*

In this Scripture, we see three levels (or degrees) of ignorance: lack of knowledge, rejection of knowledge, and forgetting knowledge or principles.

We must also not tolerate sin or any disobedience in our lives. Isa 1:19-20, makes it clear:

> *"[19] If you are willing and obedient, You shall eat the good of the land; [20] But if you refuse and rebel, You shall be devoured by the sword"; For the mouth of the LORD has spoken."*

We must not let the enemy deny or rob us of our rightful position, - that of being the Head, and not the tail, with all its benefits.

I believe God has been speaking to you as you are reading this chapter. It is now time for prayers:

First, thank God for the privilege to read His word (John 8:32; Psalm 119:130).

Thank God also for speaking to you as an individual. Thank Him in particular for His word to you and for you (Jeremiah 1:4-5)

Pray also: Father, everywhere sin has kept me from being the Head, forgive me today. Just show me mercy.

Father, if is it ignorance that has kept me from being the head, Your word has now come to me. Please make me wise to heed Your word (Psalm 119:105, 130).

Father, if it is the enemy that is at work, today, in my life and family, please destroy all the works of Satan (I John 3:7).

Father don't let me hinder You in my life. Don't let me be my own enemy.

- Today, I enter a new dawn and a new era. There is glory ahead of me. No more shame, no more failure, No more stagnation. It is forward ever and backward never!
Now, put your two hands on your own head and begin to prophesy to the organs in our head - your brain, your eyes, your ears, your mouths (lips, tongues, and teeth). Declare:
+ My brain, begin to think right. Receive Godly thoughts
+ My eyes, begin to see right - visions, open doors, help and helpers.

+   My ears, begin to hear the voice of God –the sound of abundance of rains.
+   My mouth (lips, tongues, and teeth), begin to praise God, witness for God, win souls,

-   Father, every good thing that I have lost - my health, wealth, my faith, my progress, my destiny, restore to me today, in Jesus Name.

Final Declaration: "I shall be Head, and not tail". Today, I occupy my rightful place." Please join me to pray these two very special prayer points:
-   Father, as You did to Saul of Tarsus on his way to Damascus, all who are persecuting Your Church (whether from within or from outside) turn them to promoters of Your Kingdom Agenda. If they will not yield, gently knock them down!

I pray that God will make today a positive turning point in your life and family in Jesus Name.

LET SOMEBODY SHOUT HALLELUJAH!

Chapter 1.4

Unstoppable Glory

"And Joseph said to his Brothers, "Please come near to me." So they came near. Then he said: "I am Joseph your brother, whom you sold into Egypt. But now, do not therefore be grieved or angry with yourselves because you sold me here; for God sent me before you to preserve life. For these two years the famine has been in the land, and there are still five years in which there will be neither ploughing nor harvesting. And God sent me before you to preserve a posterity for you in the earth, and to save your lives by a great deliverance. So now it was not you who sent me here, but God; and He has made me a father to Pharaoh, and lord of all his house, and a ruler throughout all the land of Egypt."

(Genesis 45:4-8)

In discussing the subject of UNSTOPPABLE GLORY, there are many personalities in the Bible that one can use as Case Studies. These include people like Joseph, Moses, Esther, Mordecai, Hannah, David, Elijah, Elisha, Daniel, the Mad man of Gadara, Peter, Paul, Timothy, etc. The best example being our Lord Jesus Christ. However, for our purpose in this Chapter, we will just take two or three - Joseph, David, and Apostle Paul. We will also take one or two testimonies from the life and Ministry of the General Overseer of the RCCG, Daddy Pastor E. A. Adeboye– my spiritual father, and also a father to many across the world.

Among other things, the word "Unstoppable" has been defined as:
Something or someone that is not able to be stopped. It is also said to be something or someone that is incapable of being stopped.

Other words for "unstoppable" are indomitable, insurmountable, unbeatable, unconquerable, invincible, etc.

In practical terms, to be stoppable means something or someone can be hindered, blocked, locked in, locked out, or locked up. It also means that a person or thing can be prevented from making progress –either upward progress, downward progress, forward or even backward. Yes, downwards or backwards, because there are times when downward or backward movements can be a progress in disguise. Someone said we must learn to retire in order to refire!

The word 'UNSTOPPABLE' is very significant. This is because it is a very important attribute of God. When it is said that God is Holy, unchangeable, reliable, dependable, etc, it is easy to understand. However, when God is said to be unstoppable, many don't really believe that truly, God is unstoppable!

God has an unlimited ability. This means nothing is difficult for Him. Also, nothing is too hard for Him. In addition, there is nothing impossible for Him to do (please see Genesis 18:14; Jeremiah 32:17, 27). One of the implications of this is that NOTHING can stop Him! Rather than being stopped by anything or anyone, God will use intending stopper as a stepping stone. I pray that all who have been trying to stop you from being who God wants you to be, or those who have been trying to hinder you from doing God's will, will become stepping stones to your promotion in Jesus Name.

There are at least three to four ways in which something or someone can be stopped:
- someone can be prevented or stopped from starting something may be a project, programme, etc.

Also, someone can be prevented from making progress on what he or she has started. In this case, he or she will be suffering stagnation, or be marking time at one point.

In addition, someone can be prevented from completing what he or she has started. In Ezra 4:4-6, we read about some attempts made to stop Ezra and his team of builders. In the book of Nehemiah, the goal of Sambalat and Tobias was to prevent Nehemiah from making progress or completing what God sent him to do. In both cases, the adversaries did all they could, but they failed. Dear reader, I pray that everything the Devil may try so that you will not make progress or finish well, will fail in Jesus Name.

Finally, someone can be prevented from enjoying what he or she has completed. God promised the Israelites in Isaiah 65:21-23:

"They shall build houses and inhabit them; They shall plant vineyards and eat their fruit. They shall not build and another inhabit; They shall not plant and another eat; For as the days of a tree, so shall be the days of My people, And My elect shall long enjoy the work of their hands. They shall not labor in vain, Nor bring forth children for trouble; For they shall be the descendants of the blessed of the Lord, And their offspring with them.".

May all these promises of our God become a reality in your life and family, and mine too in Jesus Name.

The Dictionary gave several definitions of the word 'glory'. For our purpose, we will take the one that said glory is a state of high honour, a brilliant and radiant beauty. Glory is the opposite of shame. Glory is also said to be an asset that brings praise.

When we therefore talk about "UNSTOPPABLE GLORY", it means the glory that cannot be stopped, no matter what the enemy tries. Among the cases of unstoppable glory in the Bible, we have Israel's deliverance from Egypt (Exodus Chapters 12-14). The Bible summarized this miraculous divine intervention as follows:

> *"Now the sojourn of the children of Israel who lived in Egypt was four hundred and thirty years. And it came to pass at the end of the four hundred and thirty years—on that very same day—it came to pass that all the armies of the LORD went out from the land of Egypt. It is a night of solemn observance to the LORD for bringing them out of the land of Egypt. This is that night of the LORD, a solemn observance for all the children of Israel throughout their generations."*
>
> **(Exodus 12:40-42)**

Another case is Israel's deliverance from Babylon (Psalm 126:1-6).

The most historical is the rising of Jesus from the grave after 3 days - in spite of the huge stone rolled over the entrance of the tomb, and the battalion of soldiers deployed to keep watch! (Matthew 27:62-66, Matthew 28:11-15).

This leads us to our text, which is on Joseph.
On this particular day, the jig-saw puzzle of Joseph's life came together, and suddenly, a very clear picture appeared before him. He came to realize that all he had gone through was for a purpose, and that God had been in charge all along (See Jeremiah 29:11; Romans 8:28). Two of the statements Joseph made to his Brothers are worth looking at. He told his Brothers:
> *"You sold me to Egypt". That is, "you tried to get rid of me, BUT God used it to give me a ride to the top!"*

Joseph also told his Brothers:
> *"For your information, in this very land, God has made me a father to Pharaoh, a lord of all his house and a ruler throughout all the land of Egypt."*

Each of the statuses of Joseph has it's implications. Egypt was and is still a great African country. A popular culture in many

African countries is that when a young man wakes up in the morning, he prostrates to greet his father. Thus, in addition to all that Joseph as a father to Pharaoh may mean, it is not unlikely that when it remained Joseph and Pharaoh alone in a room, someone would prostrate to the other, and Pharaoh most likely would have to. That is one of the things God can do when He makes your glory unstoppable.

That God also made Joseph a Lord of all Pharaoh's house, implies that it was Joseph who had the final say in all matters. Pharaoh himself said so in Genesis 41:44:

"without Joseph shall no man lift up his hand or foot in all the land of Egypt."

As a ruler in Egypt, Joseph was the controller General or the CEO of the national treasury of Egypt. It is often said that he who pays the piper also dictates the tune.

In summary, Joseph was saying to his Brothers: HERE I AM - THE ONE WHOSE GLORY IS UNSTOPPABLE! That will be your testimony even this year in Jesus Name.

Another person who experienced unstoppable glory was David. We find his story in I Samuel 16:7-13,18:

"But the LORD *said to Samuel, "Do not look at his appearance or at his physical stature, because I have refused him. For the* LORD *does not see as man sees; for man looks at the outward appearance, but the* LORD *looks at the heart."*

So Jesse called Abinadab, and made him pass before Samuel. And he said, "Neither has the LORD *chosen this one." ⁹ Then Jesse made Shammah pass by. And he said, "Neither has the* LORD *chosen this one." ¹⁰ Thus Jesse made seven of his sons pass before Samuel. And Samuel said to Jesse, "The* LORD *has not chosen these." ¹¹ And Samuel said to Jesse, "Are all the young men here?" Then he said, "There remains yet the youngest, and there he is, keeping the sheep." And Samuel said to Jesse, "Send and bring him. For we will not sit down till he comes here." ¹² So he sent and brought him in. Now he was ruddy, with bright eyes, and good-looking. And the* LORD *said, "Arise, anoint him; for this is the one!" ¹³ Then Samuel took the horn of oil and anointed him in the midst of his brothers; and the Spirit of the* LORD *came upon David from that day forward. So Samuel arose and went to Ramah....*

Then one of the servants answered and said, "Look, I have seen a son of Jesse the Bethlehemite, who is skillful in playing, a mighty man of valor, a man of war, prudent in speech, and a handsome person; and the LORD is with him."

David was the 8th boy in the family. From the bush one day, he was recalled home.

The fathers and brothers of Joseph and David did not reckon with them or see any greatness in them, yet God meant them for the top. Thank God that Joseph and David reached the top. You too will reach the top in Jesus Name. May God make room for you at the top in Jesus Name.
-    the battle against the destinies of the two of them was both at the home front as well as from outside. Some people think that the moment they succeed in getting out of their town, city, or nation, then the forces contending over their destinies are over. They probably don't know that Satan and demons don't know, or did not study Geography! The truth is that the only One who can free anyone from all Satanic and demonic atrocities is the Lord Jesus.

In Mark 5:1-20; and Acts 9:1-22, we find the story of two men - the Mad man of Gadarene, and Saul of Tarsus, respectively. Some things are common to the two of them. In God's Master plan, both of them were meant for greatness. The devil probably knew and was determined to prevent them from being who God wanted them to be. What did he, Satan do? He made one mad, and turned the other into a destroyer of the Church. Thank God for unstoppable glory. The two men encountered Jesus, and later fulfilled their destinies:

"Who is he who speaks and it comes to pass, When the Lord has not commanded it?. For He says to Moses, "I will have mercy on whomever I will have mercy, and I will have compassion on whomever I will have compassion." [16] So then it is not of him who wills, nor of him who runs, but of God who shows mercy."

(Lamentation 3:37; Romans 9:15-16)

Maybe you are already old or still young, and it appears the devil is all out at work in your life. Today, God will step into your situation and give you a brand new beginning in Jesus Name.

The good news is that you can be a candidate for unstoppable glory. Maybe you ask; How can I?

If you want to be a candidate for an Unstoppable like Joseph and David, or like Saul of Tarsus (who later became the renowned Apostle Paul), what must you do? All you need is to just do what Joseph, David, and all the others did. Then, you won't even need to ask God to give you what HE gave to Joseph, David, etc, it will naturally flow into your life, and men will be asking you to show them the secret.

For Joseph and David, something appeared common. That thing is: the fear of God (Please see Genesis 39:7-9, Psalm 112:1-3; Psalm 128:1-6; Proverbs 9:10-11; Proverbs 8:13, Job 1:1-2).

There is something about this thing that is called 'the fear of the Lord' - it has power to attract many things to itself, and to all who are wise to have it. The fear of God has power to attract: Divine presence, success, prosperity, mercy, favour, etc. (Genesis 39:7- 9; Psalm 112:1-3; Psalm 128:1-6).

For the Mad man of Gadarene and Saul of Tarsus, a genuine encounter with Jesus, as well as a determination to follow Him at all costs are the secrets of their UNSTOPPABLE GLORY.

A great man of God, the General Overseer of the Redeemed Christian Church of God (RCCG) Daddy G. O. once shared some of the things he went through while the Founder of the Church (RCCG) was still alive. It happened that some senior Pastors persecuted him, frustrated and tried to discourage him to the extent that he wanted to leave RCCG and join another Bible believing church. Thank God that he did not. Today, wherever he goes all over the world everyone can see the evidences of an

UNSTOPPABLE GLORY!

In Sept 2010, I was (with my wife) officially posted to the Australia/Pacific Region of the RCCG. We could not arrive there until February 2011. This was because more than twice, the Immigration refused us visa. Later a woman came up to my wife (this happened in broad daylight, and not in a dream. In fact, it was right in Church)! She told my wife all she and her evil clique were doing to 'block' our travelling. We thank God that in spite of the host of hell that ganged up, God took us there. As at the time of writing this book, by God's grace, we had spent well over TEN years in that very vast and diverse mission field!

In conclusion , let me say that UNSTOPPABLE GLORY is for those who are on the Lord's side. If you are still living in sin and you don't want to repent, glory will be far from you. Instead, you will be a candidate for shame and disgrace! "

> *"He who covers his sins will not prosper, But whoever confesses and forsakes them will have mercy."*
>
> **(Proverbs 28:13).**

This is why you must as a matter of urgency call on Jesus for help. Isaiah 55:6-7 declares:
> *"Seek the* LORD *while He may be found, Call upon*

Him while He is near. Let the wicked forsake his way, And the unrighteous man his thoughts; Let him return to the LORD *And He will have mercy on him; And to our God, For He will abundantly pardon."*

More than anything else, THERE IS AN ULTIMATE GLORY - that of reigning with JESUS. Will you and me be there? (Please see Revelation 20:11-15; Hebrew 12:14; I Corinthians 9:27).

You may want to pray as follows:
+ Father, thank You for this day of truth. Thank You for Your Word.
+ Every power that is out to stop me from fulfilling my destiny, please arrest them today - whoever, whatever, and wherever they are.

Let me throw more light on this prayer point. Many things can stop a man. For Samson, it was his eyes, for Amnon one of David's Sons, a prince, it was an evil friend, called Jonadab, who gave him an evil advice to rape his own very Sister. That singular foolish action, led to his premature death. For Gehazi and Judas, it was covetousness that put paid to their greatness. There was an Archangel, his name was Lucifer. He is more known today as Satan. It was his pride that destroyed him. Demas was another man who loved the world more than God.

Cry out once more to God: Father, anything and any power that is designed to stop me from fulling Your purpose –whoever, whatever, and wherever they are; whether inside of me, outside, or around me, please crush them today, in Jesus Name!

+ Father, please put Your fear in my heart, and help me to hate evil.
+ Father, let all who had written me off, come and prostrate for me!
+ Father, anything that will stop me from enjoying the Ultimate glory of reigning with You, please uproot from my life - both now and in my future.

In addition to the above, the following are my own personal prayers for you:
May the Lord exonerate you, and also reverse all the irreversible in your life.

As you repent, and also restitute your ways, may all your accusers fizzle out in Jesus Name.

May every urge that has been coming to you to do some things that are obviously ungodly, be uprooted from your heart in Jesus Name.

Finally, in Colossians 1:9-11, Apostle Paul prayed:
> *"For this reason we also, since the day we heard it, do not cease to pray for you, and to ask that you may be filled with the knowledge of His will in all wisdom and spiritual understanding; that you may walk worthy of the Lord, fully pleasing Him, being fruitful in every good work and increasing in the knowledge of God; strengthened with all might, according to His glorious power, for all patience and longsuffering with joy;"*

The NLT puts it this way:
> *"9 So we have not stopped praying for you since we first heard about you. We ask God to give you complete knowledge of his will and to give you spiritual wisdom and understanding. 10 Then the way you live will always honor and please the Lord, and your lives will produce every kind of good fruit. All the while, you will grow as you learn to know God better and better. 11 We also pray that you will be strengthened with all his glorious power so you will have all the endurance and patience you need. May you be filled with joy,"*

Please pray same for yourself.

OVERCOMING GIANTS

2.1 Overcoming Giants

2.2 Don't Give Up!

2.3 In Tune With God

2.4 A Stop-Over in Haran

2.5 Enough is Enough

2.6 Oh Lord, Remember Me!

Chapter 2.1

Overcoming Giants

" "And the Philistine said to David, "Come to me, and I will give your flesh to the birds of the air and the beasts of the field!"....So it was, when the Philistine arose and came and drew near to meet David, that David hurried and ran toward the army to meet the Philistine. Then David put his hand in his bag and took out a stone; and he slung it and struck the Philistine in his forehead, so that the stone sank into his forehead, and he fell on his face to the earth. So David prevailed over the Philistine with a sling and a stone, and struck the Philistine and killed him. But there was no sword in the hand of David. Therefore David ran and stood over the Philistine, took his

sword and drew it out of its sheath and killed him, and cut off his head with it. And when the Philistines saw that their champion was dead, they fled."

(I Samuel 17: 44, 48-51)

Our subject in this Chapter, from which the Book derives it's title, is "OVERCOMING GIANTS" –these are two very important words! Let's begin with 'GIANTS'

What, or who is a giant?
The word 'giant' has been variously defined as something that is very large or powerful in its effect. This definition tells us several things.

First, that a giant can be positive or negative. In other words, whatever is considered to be a giant, can be large, unusually large, good and positively powerful in it effects. On the other hand, it can also be large, unusually and largely evil, and negatively powerful in its effects! I believe a peep into human and scientific history will easily bring us in contact with personalities and inventions or endeavours that have had unusually large and powerful effects on mankind.

Second, a giant can be internal, or external. It can be open or obvious. It can be easy to identify or recognize. On the other hand, it can be subtle and hidden, operating underneath the surface.

Third, a giant can also be physical, concrete, tangible, and very visible. There are many giants that are spiritual, they cannot be seen or touched. Even here, they can be good or evil in nature or manifestation.

As a positive or good thing, a giant can be the potential or potentials in a person. A sort of redemptive gift or gifts that Is waiting to be discovered, woken up and activated. Many a man are ignorant of the great potentials God had put in them. It will take a series of divine encounters to come to this needed knowledge or realization. In Joel 3:9, we read:
> *"Proclaim this among the nations:"Prepare for war! Wake up the mighty men, Let all the men of war draw near, Let them come up."*

It took a divine awakening for someone like Gideon to realize the great potential God had put in him. Judges 6:11-14 said:
> *"Now the Angel of the LORD came and sat under the terebinth tree which was in Ophrah, which belonged to Joash the Abiezrite, while his son Gideon threshed*

wheat in the winepress, in order to hide it from the Midianites. ¹²And the Angel of the LORD appeared to him, and said to him, "The LORD is with you, you mighty man of valor!"

¹³Gideon said to Him, "O my lord, if the LORD is with us, why then has all this happened to us? And where are all His miracles which our fathers told us about, saying, 'Did not the LORD bring us up from Egypt?' But now the LORD has forsaken us and delivered us into the hands of the Midianites." ¹⁴Then the LORD turned to him and said, "Go in this might of yours, and you shall save Israel from the hand of the Midianites. Have I not sent you?"

The first in these series of divine encounters is the encounter with Jesus. It is only after a person receives Jesus that he or she begins to truly live. Such living means everything in and about you which had been dead will receive the life and Light that only Jesus can give:

"He came to His own, and His own did not receive Him. ¹²But as many as received Him, to them He gave the right to become children of God, to those who believe in His name: ¹³who were born, not of blood, nor of the will of the flesh, nor of the will of man, but of

God. [35] *The Father loves the Son, and has given all things into His hand.* [36] *He who believes in the Son has everlasting life; and he who does not believe the Son shall not see life, but the wrath of God abides on him.".* *This is the 'stone which was rejected by you builders, which has become the chief cornerstone.'* [12] *Nor is there salvation in any other, for there is no other name under heaven given among men by which we must be saved."*

(John 1:-13; John 3:35-36; Acts 4:12)

Let me clarify a little further. When we say something is dead, it means all the vital things that are evidences of life had ceased to function. For example, when a human being is said to have died, it means that all the six to seven major organs and senses are no more working- the heart had stopped beating, the ears and the eyes, are no more hearing, seeing. The person can no more relate with his or her environment or respond to stimuli. The Bible said a lot about the person of Jesus. Please see John 1:1,4-5; John 8:12; John 11:25-26; John 14:6, etc). Thus, when a person encounters or accepts Jesus as personal Saviour, Lord and King of his/her life, the life in Jesus is given to him/her. John 1: 4-5 declares:

"In Him was life, and the life was the light of men. [5]

And the light shines in the darkness, and the darkness did not comprehend it."

Jesus is the life that gives light, and the light that gives life to all men. Jesus is also the Resurrection and the Life. He has power to bring back to life anything that has died. He also has the power to stop the process of dying and decay. All He has to do is command the agents of death and their activities to cease.

As a negative thing, a giant is something that needs to be brought under control before it destroys a person's great destiny. One dictionary defined the word "GIANT" as someone or something "Monstrous and Pharaonic". That seem to me a very serious definition! Truly, a giant that is not tamed can be a monster, and a "Pharoh"!

The other word in our topic is 'overcoming'. To overcome means to defeat (someone or something). It also means to successfully deal with or gain control of (something difficult). It is said to mean affecting something or someone very strongly or severely. In short, to overcome means to conquer, to subdue, to be victorious, or to bring under control. Overcoming is far more important than just to overcome. It involves a deliberate, and continuous process, as well as the habit or efforts that ensure we keep on winning - every moment, everyday, and all our days.

- Spiritual Giants can be powers and principalities, some monuments, altars and high places. There were so many people in the Bible who faced giants. These include Lot, Jacob, Joseph, Moses, Samson, etc.

However, we will use David as a case study. In addition to our main Text, another critical Bible passage on the man David is II Samuel 12:1-9. It reads:

"Then the Lord sent Nathan to David. And he came to him, and said to him: "There were two men in one city, one rich and the other poor. The rich man had exceedingly many flocks and herds. But the poor man had nothing, except one little ewe lamb which he had bought and nourished; and it grew up together with him and with his children. It ate of his own food and drank from his own cup and lay in his bosom; and it was like a daughter to him. And a traveller came to the rich man, who refused to take from his own flock and from his own herd to prepare one for the wayfaring man who had come to him; but he took the poor man's lamb and prepared it for the man who had come to him."So David's anger was greatly aroused against the man, and he said to Nathan, "As the Lord lives, the man who has done this shall surely die! And he shall restore fourfold for the lamb, because he

did this thing and because he had no pity ." Then Nathan said to David, "You are the man! Thus says the Lord God of Israel: 'I anointed you king over Israel, and I delivered you from the hand of Saul. I gave you your master's house and your master's wives into your keeping, and gave you the house of Israel and Judah. And if that had been too little, I also would have given you much more! Why have you despised the commandment of the Lord, to do evil in His sight? You have killed Uriah the Hittite with the sword; you have taken his wife to be your wife, and have killed him with the sword of the people of Ammon."

The two passages are quite interrelated. They both reveal that during his life on earth, the great man David was confronted by two special negative giants. One was physical and human, while the other was internal.

David gallantly overcame the external and human giant by the name Goliath. However, and unfortunately, the internal giant floored king David very badly. It happened when he, David had become a very great and most powerful king in his generation. It was a great and an unfortunate historical defeat!

The story of David tells us that the internal giants may be more dangerous and terrible than the external one.

One very important thing that is common to all negative giants is that they are destiny robbers. They have a principal goal, and that goal is to kill their object or target.

In Judges 16:5-6, we read:
>"And the lords of the Philistines came up to her and said to her, "Entice him, and find out where his great strength lies, and by what means we may overpower him, that we may bind him to afflict him; and every one of us will give you eleven hundred pieces of silver." So Delilah said to Samson, "Please tell me where your great strength lies, and with what you may be bound to afflict you."

Here, Delilah did not hide her purpose!

In John 10:10, our Lord Jesus said:
>"The thief does not come except to steal, and to kill, and to destroy. I have come that they may have life, and that they may have it more abundantly"

Also, in I Peter 5:8-9, we read:
>"Be sober, be vigilant; because your adversary the devil walks about like a roaring lion, seeking whom

he may devour. Resist him, steadfast in the faith, knowing that the same sufferings are experienced by your brotherhood in the world."

The divine warning, *"be sober, be vigilant"* are very important words. To *BE* VIGILANT means to be watchful. It may also mean to be a Vigilante. In addition, it may mean to do vigil or engage in spiritual warfare at midnight. Why must we do vigil?

"Because your adversary the devil walks about like a roaring lion, seeking whom he may devour."

This passage of Scriptures gives us a very important hint about the devil. He is ever on duty (on call or patrol – 24/7)! He never goes on break and neither is he ever on holiday (see also Job 1:7). Hence we cannot afford to let down our guard.

As we said earlier, giants can be positive or negative, they can also be internal or external. Now let's look at a few internal giants. They can include: anger, unforgiveness, pride (pride of achievement -who we are, what we have, and what we have done). Internal giants may also include fear, doubt, lusts, laziness, hypocrisy, covetousness, talkativeness, greed, overeating, inordinate ambition. Each of all these had at one time or the other derailed many great destinies. They have also made some people to die prematurely. Such victims include

Moses, Vashti, Gehazi, Judas, etc, and of course, Satan himself. May none of these ever be your portion in Jesus Name.

Judas was a man who pretended that he was a holy Disciple, or one whose mind was fully with the Master. Yet, he was stealing per second, per second. Not only that he continued his scheming on how he would sell his Master.

How then do we overcome giants? Also, how can we remain overcomers to the very end of our lives, no matter the giants we face–whether external or internal, and whether physical or spiritual?

In order to overcome, there are a few important things to note and to do.

First, you must recognize that there are giants. As we said earlier in this Chapter, giants are of various types and categories.

Second, you must recognize your own giants. It may be a habit or desire. You must know where they are located in your life.

Third, you must also recognize the things that provoke, ignite, or fuel the particular giants in your life. Such things may include people, places, events, and memories.

Fourth, you must guard the gates of your life. Don't open your gates to any giant. You must watch that urge or desire! DON'T yield to it. Otherwise, it will become an open invitation for the giant to take over!

In II Corinthians 2:11, we are told:
> *"Lest Satan should get advantage of us: for we are not ignorant of his devices."*

Fifth, you must learn to weigh the consequences. The challenge here is that the devil won't want us to, or won't let us. Often, he will want to whisper to you telling you not to worry, that it's not a big deal. He may even tell you that nobody would know, or that everybody is doing it, afterall!

One of the things we must always be grateful to God for is that He has provided tools with which we can overcome any and every negative giant.

One person who God greatly helped to overcome giants, and from whom we can learn a lot, is Apostle Paul.

In Romans 7:14-25, Apostle Paul wrote:
> *"O wretched man that I am, who shall deliver me from this body of death."*

By referring to his flesh as '*body of death*', I believe he meant 'this terrible internal giant that is always with me!'

In I Corinthians 9:27, he also wrote:
> *"But I discipline my body and bring it into subjection, lest, when I have preached to others, I myself should become disqualified."*

I believe Apostle Paul is also saying two things here:
- that he would not be guilty of doing what he asked others not to do; and
- that he would not be guilty of not doing what he asked others to do.

At the end of his life, Apostle Paul gave us a testimony in II Timothy 4:6-8:
> *"For I am already being poured out as a drink offering, and the time of my departure is at hand. I have fought the good fight, I have finished the race, I have kept the faith. Finally, there is laid up for me the crown of righteousness, which the Lord, the righteous Judge, will give to me on that Day, and not to me only but also to all who have loved His appearing."*

As you are reading this book, I don't know which giant (or giants) you may have been fighting. They may be human, or institutional. They may be internal or external. Today, may God give you total and permanent victory in Jesus Name.

You may want to pray as follows:
- Father, thank You for this day of truth. You said I shall know the truth, and the Truth will set me free. I come to You right now, please help me. Deliver me from every giant that is out to ruin my life, or spoil my testimonies.
- Everything the enemy may have put in place to catch or pull me down, today destroy them.
- Father, with Your help, I possess the gates of my life - my eyes, ears, mouth, mind, feet, etc.
- Father, all the good gifts You gave me which the devil had taken over and is using to work against my destiny, I recover them today in Jesus Name.

+ Father this Year, please send me destiny helpers - from the four corners of the world and from Heaven above.

Chapter 2.1

Don't Give Up!

"Later that same day Jesus left the house and sat beside the lake." **Matthew 13:1 (NLT).**

With the help of the Holy Spirit, there are several things one can look at in this Verse. For example, we can discuss the word 'later', or the phrase 'that same day'.

Also, it could be of great benefit to talk about the Name 'Jesus', or discuss statements like 'Jesus left', 'Jesus left the house', or even 'Jesus sat'. Finally, one could look at 'He (Jesus) sat beside the lake'.

In this Chapter, we will concentrate on the phrase "later that same day, Jesus". May the Lord speak to you, even as we meditate together in Jesus Name.

Let us begin with the word or Name 'Jesus'

The Name 'JESUS' connotes a lot. For example, it is an Excellent Name. In Philippians 2:9-11, the Bible says:

> *"Therefore God also has highly exalted Him and given Him the name which is above every name, ¹⁰that at the name of Jesus every knee should bow, of those in heaven, and of those on earth, and of those under the earth, ¹¹ and that every tongue should confess that Jesus Christ is Lord, to the glory of God the Father."*

There is power in the Name of Jesus. It is the only Name that brings salvation, access to God's very presence. Miracles, and deliverance. The Bible declares:

> *"And she will bring forth a Son, and you shall call His name ⁽ᴺ⁾ JESUS, for He will save His people from their sins."..."Neither is there salvation in any other, for there is no other name under heaven given among men by which we must be saved."....¹⁵And He said to them, "Go into all the world and preach the gospel to every creature. ¹⁶ He who believes and is baptized will be*

saved; but he who does not believe will be condemned. [17] And these signs will follow those who [a]believe: In My name they will cast out demons; they will speak with new tongues; [18]they[a] will take up serpents; and if they drink anything deadly, it will by no means hurt them; they will lay hands on the sick, and they will recover."
                    (Matthew 1:21: Acts 4:12; Mark 16:16-17).

A look at the personality behind the name 'Jesus', also says alot. The same is His Words. The words of Jesus are powerful. They carry creative and restorative power:
    "It is the Spirit who gives life; the flesh profits nothing. The words that I speak to you are spirit, and they are life...."It is the Spirit who gives life; the flesh profits nothing. The words that I speak to you are spirit, and they are life."
    (John 6:63; Luke 7:11-17. See also, Mark 5:35-43).

Another thing that is worth looking at is the touch of Jesus. In Matthew 8:1-3, He touched a leprous man, and made him perfectly whole.
 One more thing we can also talk about is the mind or attitude of Jesus:
    "Let this mind be in you which was also in Christ

Jesus, who, being in the form of God, did not consider it robbery to be equal with God, but made Himself of no reputation, taking the form of a bond servant, and coming in the likeness of men. **And being found in appearance as a man, He humbled Himself and became obedient to the point of death, even the death of the cross."**

(Philippians 2:5-8).

In our text, we see Jesus moving from one place to another. Hence, we can talk about His movements (say from point A to point B), etc.

When a day starts, there are many things we plan for. Many of them may actually happen while some may not. Of course, there will be many things that we never planned or budgeted for, which may still come our way on any day.

My prayer is that for each day of your life, whether planned or not planned, only good things will be your portion in Jesus Name.

A lot can happen within a day. A day is not over until Jesus has stepped in! Hence, never give up or give in. Say to yourself, 'DON'T GIVE UP!'

A look into the lives of some people in the Bible, particularly how some days started and ended, can teach us some lessons.

Lets begin with Abraham and his wife Sarah. They woke up one day, with a great need. The couple had been trusting God for a child for over 20 years (Genesis 18:1-14). But later on, on that particular day, God showed up. About nine months later, Isaac came. Hence, I say to you too; "Don't give up"! Later today, God will show up for you in Jesus Name.

The testimony of Sarah – Abraham's wife is very instructive. A little later, the Bible said:

> *"And the LORD visited Sarah as He had said, and the LORD did for Sarah as He had spoken. For Sarah conceived and bore Abraham a son in his old age, at the set time of which God had spoken to him.* [a] *And Abraham called the name of his son who was born to him—whom Sarah bore to him—Isaac.* [a] [4]
> *Then Abraham circumcised his son Isaac when he was eight days old, as God had commanded him.* [5] *Now Abraham was one hundred years old when his son Isaac was born to him.* [6] *And Sarah said, "God has* [b] *made me laugh, and all who hear will laugh with me."* [7] *She also said, "Who would have said to Abraham that Sarah would nurse children? For I*

> *have borne him a son in his old age."*
>
> **(Genesis 21:1-7)**

One day, in Genesis 28:10-18, Jacob was on a long journey. The night came, and he slept. In his dream he encountered God. This led to a transfer of the Covenant blessings that God had earlier given to his grandfather, Abraham.

> *17 And he was afraid and said, "How awesome is this place! This is none other than the house of God, and this is the gate of heaven!" 18 Then Jacob rose early in the morning, and took the stone that he had put at his head, set it up as a pillar, and poured oil on top of it."*
>
> **(Genesis 28:17-8)**

What of Joseph? Chapter 41 of Genesis showed us that one day he woke up a prisoner, but later that day, his story changed, and he went to bed a Prime Minister (see Genesis 41: 14-16, 36-46; Genesis 37:12-24, 25-28; Genesis 39:7-20).

One day, in I Samuel 1, Hannah woke up still a barren woman. But in Vs19-21, a new and different chapter opened for her. The Bible said:

> *"Then they rose early in the morning and worshiped before the LORD, and returned and came to their house at Ramah. And Elkanah knew Hannah his wife, and*

the LORD remembered her. ²⁰So it came to pass in the process of time that Hannah conceived and bore a son, and called his name Samuel, saying, "Because I haveasked for him from the LORD."²¹

Now the man Elkanah and all his house went up to offer to the LORD the yearly sacrifice and his vow. ²²But Hannah did not go up, for she said to her husband, "Not until the child is weaned; then I will take him, that he may appear before the LORD and remain there forever."

In I Samuel 16:7-13, We read about David, then, a young shepherd boy. One day, he woke up a shepherd boy - alone in the bush, perhaps very far from the house. However, later that day, a call came from home that he must come over. That day, his story changed forever for good. Even as you read this book, I pray that before this day is over, God will show up for you and your story will change for good in Jesus Name. And if your situation is already good, it will change for the better, and even for the best in Jesus Name.

The phrase 'Later that same day, Jesus', in our opening Text, is a call to you never to give up. Don't give up on God, and don't give up on yourself!

Why must we never give up? It is because there are still a lot of good things that can still happen to you, even later today! For instance, help can still come later today. God can still bring the good news you have been expecting, later today. God can still touch and heal you, later today. God can still deliver you and set you free, later today. God can still touch that difficult husband later today. God can still touch or transfer that difficult or evil boss, later today. God can still make a way where there seems to have been none - even later today. God can still do something new, later today.

Perhaps it may be good to ask the question: **'What happened earlier that day?'** even before we start to talk about what could happen 'Later that same day'.

That portion of the Bible was a typical day in the earthly ministry of our Lord Jesus Christ, and a lot had already happened earlier in the day. You too may want to ask yourself: "What has already happened to me, earlier today?" Was it a positive or negative experience? Was it an encouraging or discouraging event or experience?

With God in the equation, He can turn situations and people around for good. He can make many good things to still happen before a day is over.

Today, may God step into your situation in Jesus Name. Let me share some personal testimonies with you.

One Sunday, several years ago, at the end of our Evening Service, I was greeting some church Elders. Then I got a tap from behind me, and a man dropped something in my hand. It was the key of a car. Earlier that day, as in many years past, I have had to get to church using commuter buses or public transport, at times up to three to four buses. BUT later that day, my story changed!

In 1997, on the Friday of our Church's Annual Convention, I woke up as usual and started participating in the day's events. Later on that day, I was invited for a meeting in the office of our General Overseer, and I received the good news of an appointment cum promotion. Earlier that day, I was a Zonal Pastor, but later that day, a good news came and my status changed. Before this day is over, may God positively change your status in Jesus Name.

On 7th Jan 2017, I woke up normally, but later in the day, a man drove in with a brand new car (Honda Civic). Initially, I thought one of our Brethren in the Church had just bought a car, and he had brought it, for a 'pastoral 'blessing'. Then he said a group of people asked him to bring the car to us as a Birthday present.

Dear Reader, it does not matter which side of the bed you woke up with this morning, I pray that before this day is over, God will visit you in Jesus Name. A testimony will come your way. God will show up for you. Before this day is over, God will arise and scatter all your enemies in Jesus Name. Jehovah will turn all your mockers to your advertisers. Psalm 126: 1-6 says:

> *"When the LORD brought back [a]the captivity of Zion, We were like those who dream.[2] Then our mouth was filled with laughter, And our tongue with singing. Then they said among the [b]nations, "The LORD has done great things for them."[3] The LORD has done great things for us, And we are glad."*

It does not matter how your past days had been, or what part of a day your life is, your latter days will be better than your former days in Jesus Name (Isaiah 1:19; Isa 3:10).

Now, God (or Jesus) stepping in, may not only be to bring miracles, it may also be to deal with the enemies, or to judge sins. Please see Judges 16:1-21; I Samuel 15: 13-23; I Samuel 17:41-51; Acts 5: 1-12.

Again, please note the phrase "LATER THAT DAY, JESUS". It means the only one who can make a positive difference between how and where a day starts, and where or how it ends is JESUS!

Why is this so? It is because of who He - Jesus is, what He has, and what He can do. Jesus is the Almighty. He is the Unchangeable Lord. He knows you and what you are going through. He is willing and ready to help you. Very importantly, He has the key of David, and when He opens a door, no one can close it. Also, when He closes a door, there is no one who can open it.

If you want each of your days to end well, and in fact be far better than how they started, you must be totally on the Lord's side. By this, I mean you must be genuinely saved. If you have not, you need to (please see Romans 3:23; Proverbs 28:13; Isaiah 55:6-7).

If you are already saved, I have an important Question for you: Are you obeying God fully, 100% ? (See Isaiah 1:19-20; Isaiah 3:10-11; Acts 10:34-35).

Dear Reader, before this day is over, I pray that God will visit you. LATER TODAY, Jesus will show up for you. Hence, DON'T GIVE UP!

In Tune With God

"Now they came to Jericho. As He went out of Jericho with His disciples and a great multitude, blind Bartimaeus, the son of Timaeus, sat by the road begging. And when he <u>heard</u> that it was Jesus of Nazareth, he began to <u>cry out and</u> say, "Jesus, Son of David, have mercy on me!" Then many warned him to be quiet; but he cried out all the more, "Son of David, have mercy on me!" So Jesus stood still and commanded him to be called. Then they called the blind man, saying to him, "Be of good cheer. Rise, He is calling you." And throwing aside his garment, he rose and came to Jesus. So Jesus answered and said to him, "What do you

want Me to do for you?" The blind man said to Him, "Rabboni, that I <u>may receive my sight</u>." Then Jesus said to him, "Go your way; your faith has made you well." And immediately <u>he received his sight and followed Jesus</u> on the road"

(Mark 10:46-52).

In this Chapter, we are discussing the crucial issue of being in tune with God. We will be answering some important Questions. For example, What does it mean to be in tune with God? Why is it important to be in tune with God? How can a person be in tune with God? What are some of the benefits of being in tune with God? Of course, we will also address practical question of how to be in tune with God, while also looking at some examples of people who were in tune with God and how they made a difference in their generations. The chapter concludes with a peep at some dangers of being out of tune with God.

To be in tune means to be in harmony. It also means to speak the same language. When two or more people are in tune with one another, it means they are operating on the same wavelength. Talking about wavelength, we are obviously living in a world of many voices. It is whatever wavelength we tune to that will determine who and what we would hear - whether our flesh, our own spirit, the voice of Satan, or the Spirit of God. I remember vividly a church Choir Leader somewhere, who, one day ended a Praise & Worship Session and asked everybody to be silent. He then said *"the Lord says I am in your midst this morning and I have accepted your worship"*. Ordinarily, nothing is wrong with the message, but in truth, it was ego boosting. A neutral person would have been better positioned to deliver such message!

The wife of a man of God woke up one morning and told her husband that the Lord was saying to her that *"henceforth, every monetary gift that came to the family must be shared 50:50!"*

In addition to our earlier definition, to be in tune also means to agree with, or to see and hear the same thing.

Since our focus is on being 'In tune with God', what does this involve? What exactly does it mean to be in tune with God?

To be in tune with God among other things means to see as God sees. Our God is a seeing God. He is not blind. In Psalm 94:7-12, we read:

> *"Yet they say,"The LORD does not see, Nor does the God of Jacob understand." Understand, you senseless among the people; And you fools, when will you be*

> *wise?* He who planted the ear, shall He not hear? He who formed the eye, shall He not see?
> He who instructs the nations, shall He not correct? He that teacheth man knowledge, shall He not know?" The LORD knows the thoughts of man, That they are futile." Blessed is the man whom You instruct, O Lord. And teach out of Your law"

In fact, God's eyes are very sharp and penetrating. He sees in great details (II Chronicles 16:9)

The Question then is, How does God see? Well, the Bible gave us some clue:
First, God does not see as men see. I Samuel 16:7; Isaiah 55:8-9 declare:

> "But the LORD said to Samuel, "Do not look at his appearance or at his physical stature, because I have refused him. For the LORD does not see as man sees; for man looks at the outward appearance, but the LORD looks at the heart."…."For My thoughts are not your thoughts, Nor are your ways My ways," says the LORD. "For as the heavens are higher than the earth, So are My ways higher than your ways, And My thoughts than your thoughts."

Second, God sees all - He is the all-seeing, and al- knowing God -

- the Omniscient One)! He sees the end from the beginning. He is the Alpha and Omega:

> *"I am the Alpha and the Omega, the Beginning and the End," says the Lord, "who is and who was and who is to come, the Almighty."*
>
> **(Revelation 1:8).**

God also sees in the day as well as in the night (In addition, He sees in secret. Of course, He also rewards in the open:

> *"[11] If I say, "Surely the darkness shall fall on me," Even the night shall be light about me;[12] Indeed, the darkness shall not hide from You, But the night shines as the day; The darkness and the light are both alike to You. But when you do a charitable deed, do not let your left hand know what your right hand is doing, that your charitable deed may be in secret; and your Father who sees in secret will Himself reward you openly. "And when you pray, you shall not be like the hypocrites. For they love to pray standing in the synagogues and on the corners of the streets, that they may be seen by men. Assuredly, I say to you, they have their reward. But you, when you pray, go into your room, and when you have shut your door, pray to your Father who is in the secret place; and your Father who sees in secret will reward you openly."*

(Psalm 139:10-12; Matthew 6:3- 6).

God sees with eternity in view, and He sees us as individuals. Finally and also very importantly, God sees with the eye of love and mercy.

Thus, to be in tune with God means to see and/or hear the same thing that God sees and hears.

Being in tune with God also implies being in touch with Him. This is beyond just seeing or hearing from Him but in particular being current and up-to-date with Him.

It is important and of great advantage to be in tune with God. In fact, is it a MUST to be in tune with God! The benefits are many.

First, the uncertainties of life are so many. Hence every man or woman needs God's direction/leading, otherwise, we would all become food for the lions! In John 10:10; I Peter 5:5-8, we read:
> *"The thief does not come except to steal, and to kill, and to destroy. I have come that they may have life, and that they may have it more abundantly." "I am the good shepherd. The good shepherd gives His life for the sheep.". " casting all your care upon Him, for He cares for you.*

> *Be sober, be vigilant; because your adversary the devil walks about like a roaring lion, seeking whom he may devour. Resist him, steadfast in the faith, knowing that the same sufferings are experienced by your brotherhood in the world."*

Second, the enemies and forces we cannot or can never see operate all around us – both in the day, and especially at night (See Psalm 91:1-10; Ephesians 6:10-18; II Corinthians 10:3-5)

Third, it is dangerous (if not suicidal) to be out of tune with God. The experiences of some 'executive' backsliders (like Samson, King David, Lucifer), show how dangerous it could be.

Fourth, God is interested in the details of our lives. As a loving Father, He does not want us to go astray, be wounded or maimed, or even suffer any calamity before we reach our goals and fulfil destiny.

In terms of benefits, the examples of Moses, the Sons of Issachar, Peter, as well as others in the Bible, show how helpful it is to be in tune with God. (Please see Psalm 103:7; I Chronicles 12:32; Matthew 16:22-23)

What are we to do to be in tune with God- not occasionally but all the time (24/7)?

First, we need to understand how this Great God operates. The Bible describes God as Sovereign, and Unquestionable (Psalm 115:3; Psalm 135:6; Daniel 4:35). Nevertheless, it is very important to point out that God is never arbitrary in His utterances and actions. He is a God of principles, and He is very orderly. Also, God has His agenda and time table – both for events, people, nations, and even generations (Genesis 12:1-3; Genesis 15:7-16).

Second, we must know that there are some things God is not in a hurry about. In such situations and cases, He shows His Royalty or Sovereignty by taking His time to do thorough preparations. For example, the coming of Christ into the world. The same with the birth of Isaac and his grandson; Joseph. Of course, there are some cases in which God is in a great hurry - because of the good He wants to accomplish. In such a case, anyone/anything that want to hinder/stop Him will become a stepping stone to help Him get the results He desires. (Psalm 76: 10, NLT).

Third, there is the need to recognize God's voice. I call it "The First Voice". We have to cultivate the art of listening <u>to</u>, and listening <u>for</u> His Voice.
The Bible is the Word of God. As we read or hear the Scriptures,

we should know that it is God speaking to us:

> *[16] All Scripture is inspired by God and is useful to teach us what is true and to make us realize what is wrong in our lives. It corrects us when we are wrong and teaches us to do what is right. [17] God uses it to prepare and equip his people to do every good work."*
>
> **(II Tim 3:16-17, NLT)**

Now, the Word of the Scriptures had been described as the "Logos". As we personalize the Word and make it applicable to our individual situation or circumstances, it becomes 'the Word of God to us and for us', which has been termed a "Rhema".

Fourth, we are to see as God sees, and also see what He sees. The Bible tells us about how God sees (again, please see I Samuel 16:7; II Chronicles 19:9; Matthew 6:4,6; Psalm 19:10-11).

Finally, we must totally surrender to God, and have the right priorities (Matthew 6:33).

Who can be in tune with God?

It is only those who, among other things, are in the spirit (John 4:23-24; John 6:63); have God's mind & attitude (Philippians 2:5-8; I Corinthians 2:9-14; I Samuel 16:7); are willing and ready to obey God's voice and directives (Isaiah 1:19)

- agree with God - that He is the Portal and he or she the mortal;
- agree that God's plans are right and superior - the best from a loving Father (Amos 3:3), and,
- are not seeking self glory but God's glory (Acts 8:32-39),

There are several personalities who knew what it meant to be in tune with God. They include the Old Testament Prophets, David, Apostle Paul, and our Lord Jesus Christ, among others. (Pease see I Samuel 23:1-5; Jeremiah 1;4-5; I Kings 18;37-39; Isaiah 6;1-8).

Am I in tune with God? Is it possible to know if I am in tune with God? The answer is Yes! If I'm in tune with God, how can I stay in tune? To be in tune with God, and also stay connected, we must:
- continually be obedient to His instructions to us (John 8:29; Genesis 39: 7-9). This means being sensitive to His Holy Spirit as He gently prompts us on what to do. It could be in small or simple day to day things like what to wear, what to say, where to go or not to go, etc.

Let me share a few instances with us:

Not too long ago, I was at a church programme as a Guest Speaker. As I arrived in the auditorium and settled down, I glanced through the Order of Service. I perceive the Holy Spirit saying to me that the Word ministration should come up earlier (rather than much later as stated on the paper. Ordinarily, wherever I go I subject myself to the authority of whoever invited me. But on this day, things seemed different. So, I whispered to my host senior pastor to reorder the programme so we could have the Word Ministration before High Praise/music and dances! We thank God that everything went well, and God was greatly glorified. Later, the Pastor came to thank me for it, saying the decision was clearly of God.

Several years ago, in a Low-cost Housing Estate, I was on a House-to-House Evangelism. On the staircase in one of the Blocks, I ran into a young Moslem boy. I stretched my hand to give him a Gospel leaflet (TRACT). He violently rebuffed me, shouting "Leave me alone, I'm a Moslem!" Though he appeared young and feeble, his resistance was extra-ordinary, I felt flatly defeated. However, right there and then, I prayed and perceived the Lord urging me to go and ask him just one question: "Has your religion delivered you from sin?" I ran down the staircase, and met him trying to gather some clothes from off the wire. I told him that I recognized that he was a Moslem, but that I had a question for him – "Has your religion delivered you from sin?" This time, to my surprise, the boy became quiet, and more or less went blank! At the end, he took more than two of the leaflets!

If and when a man or woman is in tune with God, he will be blessed, and he or she will be a blessing. The reverse is also true: When a person is out of tune with God, he or she will be an offence to God and His Kingdom Agenda!

Of course, he or she will also be an offense rather than a blessing to his or her generation.

What are all these telling us?: There is a wall of difference between being in tune with God and being in tune with man or with men. It is possible to be in tune with men and be seriously out of tune with God! On the other hand, it is possible to be in tune with God and seriously out of tune with men.

Only a discerning mind or heart can know the difference. A man of God was on a trip and he ended up worshipping in a church. According to him, everything was 'gym-gym', but he said he heard God saying very clearly; "I AM NOT IN ALL THESE". After the Service, he went to meet the pastor. He complimented him for all the 'great work'. He then politely told the pastor what God had said to him. The pastor said he knew God was not in all they were doing. Then the Pastor shocked the visitor further with the statement: *'in this church, when God does not move, we move!*

My prayer is that may we stay in tune with God and get divine instructions that will accelerate the fulfilment of our destinies in Jesus Name. May we become a blessing both to God's Kingdom and to our generation in Jesus Name, Amen.

Chapter 2.4

A Stop Over in Haran

"And Terah took his son Abram and his grandson Lot, the son of Haran, and his daughter-in-law Sarai, his son Abram's wife, and they went out with them from Ur of the Chaldeans to go to the land of Canaan; and they came to Haran and dwelt there. So the days of Terah were two hundred and five years, and Terah died in Haran....Now the Lord had said to Abram: "Get out of your country, From your family And from your father's house, To a land that I will show you. I will make you a great nation; I will bless you And make your name great; And you shall be a blessing. I will bless those who bless you, And I will curse him who curses you; And in you all the families of the

earth shall be blessed." So Abram departed as the Lord had spoken to him, and Lot went with him. And Abram was seventy-five years old when he departed from Haran. Then Abram took Sarai his wife and Lot his brother's son, and all their possessions that they had gathered, and the people whom they had acquired in Haran, and they departed to go to the land of Canaan. So they came to the land of Canaan."
(Genesis 11:31-32, 12:1-5).

In the above Text, we see a family embarking on a journey. The family is made up of three generations-the Grandfather called Terah, his son Abraham and his wife, as well as a grandson named Lot. They all started well, but a little over half of the journey, they had a stop over in a city called Haran.

Though we are not told for how long they were in Haran, the Bible went on that Terah; the Grandfather died in Haran. The rest of the family however continued.

In this Chapter, we shall be looking at four questions:
- why the stop over in Haran?
- what did the stop over lead to?
- Are there any 'Harans' in my way?

A Stop Over in Haran

- Have I stopped or am I planning to stop over in Haran?

Let me reiterate the fact that God has a great purpose for every person He had made. There is a place He planned to take us – those of us who are His true children, and it is a glorious place – both here on earth, and also in the eternity to come - there is a place He is taking us:

> "⁴ *Then the word of the* LORD *came to me, saying: "Before I formed you in the womb I knew you; Before you were born I sanctified⁽ᵃ⁾ you; I ⁽ᵇ⁾ordained you a prophet to the nations."…."* ¹¹*For I know the thoughts that I think toward you, says the* LORD, *thoughts of peace and not of evil, to give you a future and a hope….⁹But as it is written: "Eye has not seen, nor ear heard, Nor have entered into the heart of man, The things which God has prepared for those who love Him."* ¹⁰*But God has revealed them to us through His Spirit. For the Spirit searches all things, yes, the deep things of God.* ¹¹*For what man knows the things of a man except the spirit of the man which is in him? Even so no one knows the things of God except the Spirit of God.* ¹²*Now we have received, not the spirit of the world, but the Spirit who is from God, that we*

might know the things that have been freely given to us by God."
(Jeremiah 1:4-5; Jeremiah 29:11; I Corinthians 2:9-12).

In our Text, God told Abraham where He wants to take Him - Greatness. God also told him what he needed to do. Abraham took some people with Him or found himself surrounded by some people he could not humanly speaking easily cut off from. As we earlier mentioned, they started well, but after some time, they decided to stop over in Haran.

Why the stop over in Haran?
It could be for some reasons: It could be to take some rest - Every journey has it's challenges, its ups and downs, curves and bends. These challenges could weary us down and out. So, they may have stopped over in Haran to take some rests, and to refresh themselves. Ordinarily there is nothing evil in this. However, when some rests are taken prematurely, or at the wrong place, it may become a snare, with some negative consequences in I Kings 13:1-end, is the story of a young Prophet on a God-given assignment. He decided to rest prematurely or at a wrong place – all against God's instructions to him. The end result was his premature death! May God have mercy upon us all.

Abram and his Team may also have stopped in Haran to experience some of the attractions of the city. Unfortunately, the attractions became distractions and a trap!

What did the stop over lead to?
First, Terah, Abram's father never made it to Canaan! He died in Haran. One can imagine the stress and all that Terah's death in a place where they were all strangers could have caused.

Second, Abraham - a man with a definite call of God upon his life with his wife wasted some precious time and resources in Haran.

What are all these telling us?:
It costs more to be in the wrong place than to be in the right place. No matter how brief, when you are in the wrong place, it is most likely you will be in the wrong company. You are most likely to see, hear, think and even do the wrong things (Psalm 1:1; Judges 16:1-21; II Samuel 11:1-5, 6-17; Luke 22: 54-61; I Thessalonians 5:22).

Furthermore, you will surely miss out on some blessings. The opportunities and privileges of being at the right place at the right time will elude you.
> *"For the* LORD *God is a sun and shield; The* LORD *will give grace and glory; No good thing will He withhold*

From those who walk uprightly."

(Psalm 84:11)

Are there any 'Harans' in my way?
+ For Abraham and team, Haran was a place of temporary rest that turned out to be a death trap. It was a means to an end that turned out to become an end in itself.
+ Haran can be a person who is luring you into sin - a boss, a colleague, a subordinate, etc.
+ Haran may be a seducing spirit in your office, your neighbourhood or college.
+ Haran may also be that comfort zone that is giving you the impression that you have arrived - that little success that is intoxicating you, and making you to feel that there is no one like you!
+ Of course, Haran may be that hurt, or disappointment you saw in the service of God, that made you to conclude that it is not worth serving God any more (Malachi 2:14-18)
+ Haran may also be a discouragement or hardship in your studies, marriage, or life in general, and you think it is better to quit or end it all.
+ Haran may be something inside or around you that is resisting or rebelling against the will of God.

Dear Reader, where are you in your own journey of life? Have you stopped over, or are you planning to stop over in Haran? You are the only one who can answer that in I Corinthians 10:12- 13; I Corinthians 13:5-8, the Bible says:

> *"[12] If you think you are standing strong, be careful not to fall. [13] The temptations in your life are no different from what others experience. And God is faithful. He will not allow the temptation to be more than you can stand. When you are tempted, he will show you a way out so that you can endure..... [5] or rude. It does not demand its own way. It is not irritable, and it keeps no record of being wronged. [6] It does not rejoice about injustice but rejoices whenever the truth wins out. [7] Love never gives up, never loses faith, is always hopeful, and endures through every circumstance. [8] Prophecy and speaking in unknown languages[a] and special knowledge will become useless. But love will last forever!*

Let me conclude with these Questions:
- Will you reach your own Canaan at all?
- will you reach it intact or with some scandal and scars?

It's time to pray:
- Father, thank You for Your Master plan for my life. Thank

You for helping me so far.
- Every agenda of the enemy concerning my life, please tear into pieces.
- Everything Satan has put in place to derail me or prevent me from reaching my own Canaan, Father roast them in Your Fire.
- Every road block to reaching my destiny, Father dismantle.
- If I have already stopped over or settled down in Haran, Father, break me loose. With Your Help, I pack my load and resume my journey to my destiny.
- Father, as You take me out of Haran, please take Haran out of me! (Remember Moses!–he was out of Egypt but Egypt was still in and all over him - Exodus 2: 16-20).
- Father, please help me, don't let me die in Haran? Let me reach my goal, and fulfil my purpose.

Chapter 2.5

Enough is Enough!

"1 Now Moses kept the flock of Jethro his father in law, the priest of Midian: and he led the flock to the backside of the desert, and came to the mountain of God, even to Horeb. 2 And the angel of the LORD appeared unto him in a flame of fire out of the midst of a bush: and he looked, and, behold, the bush burned with fire, and the bush was not consumed. 3 And Moses said, I will now turn aside, and see this great sight, why the bush is not burnt. 4 And when the LORD saw that he turned aside to see, God called unto him out of the midst of the bush, and said, Moses, Moses. And he said, Here am I. 5 And he said, Draw not nigh hither: put off thy shoes from off thy feet, for the place whereon thou standest is holy ground. 6 Moreover he said, I am the God of thy father, the God of

Abraham, the God of Isaac, and the God of Jacob. And Moses hid his face; for he was afraid to look upon God. 7 And the LORD said, I <u>have surely seen</u> the <u>affliction</u> of my people which are in Egypt, and <u>have heard their cry</u> by reason of their taskmasters; for I know their sorrows; 8 And <u>I am come down to deliver</u> them out of the hand of the Egyptians, <u>and to bring them up</u> out of that land <u>unto a good land and a large, unto a land flowing with milk and honey;</u> unto the place of the Canaanites, and the Hittites, and the Amorites, and the Perizzites, and the Hivites, and the Jebusites. 9 Now therefore, behold, the cry of the children of Israel is come unto me: <u>and I have also seen the oppression</u> wherewith the Egyptians oppress them.10 Come now therefore, and I will send thee unto Pharaoh, that thou mayest bring forth my people the children of Israel out of Egypt."

(Exodus 3:1-10).

In this Chapter, we shall be discussing our subject - "Enough is Enough", from about four perspectives: The first is in relation to complacency and Contentment.

There are some people who are often satisfied with the minimum - minimum joy, minimum blessing, minimum promotion, etc. They are comfortable with the average or even less than average! A little is just enough for them. All they aim at is just to make ends meet! They say God asked them to be contented. Dear Reader, are you among such people? May I tell you that **THERE IS A WALL OF DIFFERENCE BETWEEN "CONTENTMENT" and "COMPLACENCY"**!

Why must you be satisfied or complacent with the minimum when God wants you to have the maximum? Why must you be satisfied with where or what you have when there is a higher and better place God has in mind for you?

Without any doubt, God wants His children to be contented, as His word says in I Timothy 6:6-7, and Psalm 37:16:

"Now godliness with contentment is great gain. For we brought nothing into this world, and it is certain we can carry nothing out... A little that a righteous man has Is better than the riches of many wicked."

However, God hates complacency! The reason is obvious: Complacency is a waste of His deposits in us (See Matthew 25:29-31).

Through complacency or comfort of the present, we often limit ourselves. Worse still, we even limit God. Someone said 'good is the enemy of best'. Apostle Paul was a man who hated complacency. In Philippians 3:12-14, he said:

> *"Not that I have already attained, or am already perfected; but I press on, that I may lay hold of that for which Christ Jesus has also laid hold of me. Brethren, I do not count myself to have apprehended; but one thing I do, forgetting those things which are behind and reaching forward to those things which are ahead, I press toward the goal for the prize of the upward call of God in Christ Jesus."*

Please join in praying as follows:

+ Father, deliver me from every evil complacency. Take me forward - Open my eyes, let me begin to see and desire great things. -
+ Father, every embargo or limitation over my rising - whether physically or spiritually, uproot in Jesus Name.
+ Father, Open my eyes, let me begin to see great things–great opportunities and open doors.
+ Father, please enlarge my coast, and connect me with destiny helpers.
+ Father, please make me great, and don't let me die small.

The second perspective of 'Enough is Enough' is that of a Miracle seed.

Many people often look at the magnitude of the challenges they face and forget the greatness, of their God. They forget that God is the ALMIGHTY, and that with Him nothing shall be impossible. Such people also forget that God has enough power to make a way where there appears to be none, and that He can bring something out of nothing, while He is also able to turn a little to much. Such people in fact forget that the Sovereign God is the King of kings, and the Lord of lords.

In and around us, this awesome God has placed a miracle seed - something that is just enough for Him to use to trigger off or connect us with our miracles. But very often, we ignore, underrate or even overlook such seeds.

In II Kings 4:1-7, a Widow was in a huge debt. The debt was so huge that her creditors threatened to take her two sons in lieu of what she owed. Rather than accept her lot, she ran to a man of God who asked if she had anything in the house that God could use as a miracle seed. Initially, she overlooked her small bottle of oil, and told the man of God, Prophet Elisha that she had nothing! At the end she zeroed in on her small bottle of oil, which became a miracle seed. She returned home and diligently followed the instructions of the man of God. The God who has power to turn little into much, multiplied the oil and caused it to flow and overflow until it filled several jars! She went back to the prophet who further instructed her to sell the oil to pay her debt, and live on the rest. Before this day is over, may the Lord surprise you for good in Jesus Name.

In John 6:8-12, we see a typical day in the ministry of the Lord Jesus. The Lord fed well over 5,000 people with a young Boy's Lunch pack. It was a miracle seed.

Please join in praying as follows:
+ Father, today, not tomorrow, level up every obstruction to my progress - whether human, institutional, or financial.
+ Father, You know me in and out, You know where the shoe is pinching me, please today, <u>oil and lubricate</u> my life. Put an end to every struggle, every friction, every hardship in my life.
+ That little seed in my hand, turn it to a mighty instrument for my breakthrough.
+ Father, Open my eyes to solutions - destiny helpers, resources, talents and gifts which You have put around me.

Thirdly, 'Enough is Enough' can be discussed in relation to Divine turnaround. We can also call this **"A New Beginning"**. In this perspective, we shall illustrate with several people and situations in the Bible:

A Divine Turnaround can come by God making a way where there was none before," In Exodus 14: 27- 31, we read:

> *"And Moses stretched out his hand over the sea; and when the morning appeared, the sea returned to its full depth, while the Egyptians were fleeing into it. So the Lord overthrew the Egyptians in the midst of the sea. Then the waters returned and covered the chariots, the horsemen, and all the army of Pharaoh that came into the sea after them. Not so much as one of them remained. But the children of Israel had walked on dry land in the midst of the sea, and the waters were a wall to them on their right hand and on their left. So the Lord saved Israel that day out of the hand of the Egyptians, and Israel saw the Egyptians dead on the seashore. Thus Israel saw the great work which the Lord had done in Egypt; so the people feared the Lord, and believed the Lord and His servant Moses."*

- A Divine Turnaround can also come by way of a divine elevation. This was the experience of Joseph and also, David. In Genesis 41:14-37, God moved Joseph from the Prison to the throne - (not just from prison to the palace). In I Samuel 16:7-13, David was promoted from a shepherd boy to being the King of Israel - the greatest king of all times!

•   Divine Turnaround can also come by way of God mocking all your mockers. In I Samuel 1: 10-21, we find the story of Hannah - she was initially barren, but God stepped in, and made her fruitful. You may not be physically barren, but there may be an area of life where the enemy is mocking you. In Psalm 137:1-4, we read:

> *"By the rivers of Babylon, There we sat down, yea, we wept When we remembered Zion. We hung our harps Upon the willows in the midst of it. For there those who carried us away captive asked of us a song, And those who plundered us requested mirth, Saying, "Sing us one of the songs of Zion!" How shall we sing the Lord's song In a foreign land?"*

A man had a young Brother-in-Law who used to call him by a derogatory name. One way or the other, the in-law heard that the man's daughter was wedding. So, he decided to go and see. At the occasion, God was at work, and the young man later prostrated to greet the man.

Please join in praying as follows:
+   Father, today, please do something in my life to silence and mock all my mockers.
+   Father, very soon, let all my mockers come and prostrate for me.

\+   Father, very soon, let all who say there is no hope for me know that You have not finished with me.

I join my faith with yours: Today, God will silence and disgrace all who have been mocking you and asking where is your God in Jesus Name.

The fourth and final dimension of 'Enough is enough' we want to consider is in relation to Spiritual warfare.

In our main Text (Exodus 3:1-10), we see God saying "<u>Enough is Enough</u>" to those who had been holding His people to ransom, and preventing them from fulfilling their purpose, or reaching their destiny.

In Vs 7-9, God said to Moses: "*I have seen, I have heard, I know, and I have come down*". Here, God seem to be saying" I can't stand it any more", "enough is enough to all the enemy had been doing". "I'm ready to intervene!"(Isaiah 40:1-2). I perceive God is saying concerning your situations, "ENOUGH IS ENOUGH"!

\+   What is God saying to that sickness in your body," ENOUGH IS ENOUGH"!

To that failure: - "ENOUGH IS ENOUGH" - No more failure.

To that Barrenness, "ENOUGH IS ENOUGH! - No more barrenness.

To that Disappointment and Stagnation, "ENOUGH IS ENOUGH"! Your time of favour has come. Prepare for your next level - marriage, promotion, open doors (Psalm 102:13).

To every area where you have been experiencing Shame and calamities, God is saying to that Shame and calamity, "ENOUGH IS ENOUGH! No more shame, no more calamity (Numbers 23:21).

Dear Reader, "Enough is enough is a call to arms. It is an invitation to spiritual warfare. It is a call to resist and rebuke the arch enemy. It is a call to summon your Ally - Jehovah the Man of war!

Please join in praying as follows
+ Every pursuer of my life - whether physically or spiritually (in my dreams), Father pursue them!
+ Father, arise and let every enemy of my destiny be scattered!

+   Father, everywhere I go, let helpers seek me out to help me.
+   Father, I decree right now "ENOUGH IS ENOUGH" to every negative story of my life. (You may want to add other prayer points).

In conclusion, the One who said "ENOUGH IS ENOUGH" to what the enemy was doing in the lives of His Children in the Passage we read, is also the One who is saying to you right now: Enough of a life of sin (Romans 6:1-2; Proverbs 28:13; Isa 55:6-7). Please, don't ignore His warning, (kindly go and read Proverbs 1:24-33 - the reward is there)! I appeal to you to <u>BE WISE</u> and come to Jesus right now - before it is too late.

Perhaps, dear reader, you know clearly that God has a definite thing He wants to use you for, but you have been running away, you have been listening to and following the counsel of the wicked! I believe God is giving you another chance, don't delay further.

Chapter 2.6

"O Lord, Remember Me"

"Then Samson called to the Lord, saying, "O Lord God, remember me, I pray! Strengthen me, I pray, just this once, O God, that I may with one blow take vengeance on the Philistines for my two eyes!" And Samson took hold of the two middle pillars which supported the temple, and he braced himself against them, one on his right and the other on his left. Then Samson said, "Let me die with the Philistines!" And he pushed with all his might, and the temple fell on the lords and all the people who were in it. So the dead that he killed at his death were more than he had killed in his life. And his brothers and all his father's house hold came down and took him, and brought

him up and buried him between Zorah and Eshtaol in the tomb of his father Manoah. He had judged Israel twenty years."

(Judges 16:28-31).

et's begin our discussion with two very important Questions: Which one is older - what you are going through as a human being, or the Word of God?

Which one must bow to the other - your situation and challenges (on one hand), or the Word of God (on the other)?

Dear reader, may I inform you that God has a word that He has designed and written to attend to every situation you face in life - even before the situations arise. The situation could be a need in your body, by way of health challenges. It may be in your career, your finances, or your relationships. It may be in your Ministry, or even your Nation.

All that is needed is for you to receive the appropriate WORD that you need from God. You also need to activate such word by faith. When this happens, your miracles will be in your hands.

You may want to pray right away as follows:
- Father, please speak to me as I read this chapter.
- Father, Your Word is spirit and life; Your Word is quick and sharp. Please send Your Word to change my situation for good, today.

Remember me Oh Lord' is a passionate and personal call, as well as prayer from man to God. Why such a call? Why call upon God to remember you? I believe the answer is not far fetched. The only One who can truly help us is God Himself. Men may know us, but in critical times they may not remember us! Men may even remember us in times of need but may be unable to help us. This can be for several reasons. For instance, they may not know our needs. They may even know our needs but may not have the capacity to help. There are times when men may know our needs and they may have the capacity to help but may be unable to help us because they have their own pressing problems.

I once heard the story of a woman who always went to a man of God. After each narrative on what she had been going through (in the enemies' hands), she would burst into tears and weep unending. Then one day, she went as usual to the same man of God but noted how moody and downcast the man of God was. She asked him if all was well. Rather than answer her in words, the man of God burst into tears! Apparently he too had been overwhelmed by some recent challenges in his own family. That was the last time the woman went to bother the man of God with her own troubles. What does the Bible admonish us to do?:

> *"Therefore we also, since we are surrounded by so great a cloud of witnesses, let us lay aside every weight, and the sin which so easily ensnares us, and let us run with endurance the race that is set before us, looking unto Jesus, the author and finisher of our faith, who for the joy that was set before Him endured the cross, despising the shame, and has sat down at the right hand of the throne of God."*
>
> **(Hebrews 12:1-2)**

One of the many attributes of God is that He is all-knowing. He does not and can not forget His people or His promises. The Bible says:

> *""Known to God from eternity are all His works."*
>
> **(Acts 15:18)**

A call to God to remember is therefore a call that He should please step into a matter or case, and accelerate action. In the Bible, there were several people in unpleasant situations. At the end of the day, we read that God remembered them. By that it is meant that God stepped into their cases and changed their story for good. For example, the woman called Hannah. The Bible said in I Samuel 1:1-2, 6-7, 10-11, 17-20:

"Now there was a certain man of Ramathaim Zophim, of the mountains of Ephraim, and his name was Elkanah the son of Jeroham, the son of Elihu, the son of Tohu, the son of Zuph, an Ephraimite. ²And he had two wives: the name of one was Hannah, and the name of the other Peninnah. Peninnah had children, but Hannah had no children...And her rival also provoked her severely, to make her miserable, because the LORD had closed her womb. ⁷So it was, year by year, when she went up to the house of the LORD, that she provoked her; therefore she wept and did not eat... And she was in bitterness of soul, and prayed to the LORD and wept in anguish. Then she made a vow and said, "O LORD of hosts, if You will indeed look on the affliction of Your maidservant and remember me, and not forget Your maidservant, but will give Your maidservant a male child, then I will give him to the LORD all the days of his life, and no razor shall come upon his head."...Then Eli answered and said, "Go in peace, and the God of Israel grant your petition which you have asked of Him." ¹⁸And she said, "Let your maidservant find favor in your sight." So the woman went her way and ate, and her face was no longer ¹⁹ *Then they rose early in the morning*

andworshiped before the LORD, *and returned and came to their house at Ramah. And Elkanah knew Hannah his wife, and the* LORD *remembered her.* ²⁰*So it came to pass in the process of time that Hannah conceived and bore a son, and called his name Samuel, saying, "Because I have asked for him from the* LORD.*""*

(Please, also see Genesis 30:1-2, 22-24).

'Remember me Oh Lord' is also a call to God to show mercy. Many times, the man David made that call.

Remember me Oh Lord', can be a call to God asking Him to deal with the forces that will not let us be who and where God want us to be. Psalm 68:1-2, says:

"Let God arise, Let His enemies be scattered; Let those also who hate Him flee before Him. ²*As smoke is driven away, So drive them away; As wax melts before the fire, So let the wicked perish at the presence of God."*

As many people in the Bible called upon God to remember them, and HE did; My prayer for you is that as you too call upon Him today, He will remember you and answer you by fire in Jesus Name.

It is notable that some people will not call upon God to remember them. Some in this category may actually be people who stopped calling on God because they have been overwhelmed by situations, and had given up on God, accepting what they term as their fate. I pray that evil will never be your fate in Jesus Name. It will not be mine too in Jesus Name, Amen! The Bible declares:

> *"He has not observed iniquity in Jacob, Nor has He seen [a]wickedness in Israel. The LORD his God is with him, And the shout of a King is among them.* [22] *God brings them out of Egypt; He has strength like a wild ox.* [23] *"For there is no [b]sorcery against Jacob, Nor any [c]divination against Israel. It now must be said of Jacob And of Israel, 'Oh, what God has done!'"*

This takes us back to our main Text which we read earlier (Judges 16:28-31). It is the story of Samson.

Who was Samson? He was a child of destiny (COD). There were many children of destiny in the Bible. They included Isaac, Joseph, Moses, Esther, Samuel, David, John the Baptist, etc. Like many children of destiny, Samson's birth was delayed (at least from man's limited understanding). He was born to a couple who were initially barren - Mr Manoah and wife (please see Judges 13:1-end).

Apart from John the Baptist and our Lord Jesus Christ, Samson was probably the only person in the Bible who had a great detail of his birth foretold. God had a special assignment for him. To enable him function, God specially anointed him right from the womb. In Judges 13:1-5, we read:

> *"Again the children of Israel did evil in the sight of the Lord, and the Lord delivered them into the hand of the Philistines for forty years. Now there was a certain man from Zorah, of the family of the Danites, whose name was Manoah; and his wife was barren and had no children. And the Angel of the Lord appeared to the woman and said to her, "Indeed now, you are barren and have borne no children, but you shall conceive and bear a son. Now therefore, please be careful not to drink wine or similar drink, and not to eat anything unclean. For behold, you shall conceive and bear a son. And no razor shall come upon his head, for the child shall be a Nazirite to God from the womb; and he shall begin to deliver Israel out of the hand of the Philistines."*

Samson did many exploits for God, but he was not careful to watch out for some destiny destroyers in his own life. He went in into women of all shades. Then came Delilah into his life. Delilah became Samson's albatross. At the end of the day, Samson released the secret of his greatness to Delilah, and she scraped Samson's head. Delilah later called in the Philistines who gorged out Samson's two eyes, and got him chained. He was then led away and became a grinder of corn in the shrine of the Philistines – the very enemies God had raised him up to destroy! Vs 28 of our Text says:

> *"Then Samson called to the Lord, saying, "O Lord God, remember me, I pray! Strengthen me, I pray, just this once, O God, that I may with one blow take vengeance on the Philistines for my two eyes!"*

Here, Samson prayed a desperate prayer! Thank God that Samson remembered God in his time of trouble. He called upon God for help. All along, Samson had probably thought he was strong to handle situations - all by himself, after all, the anointing was there. In Psalm 30:6-7, King David said:

> *"Now in my prosperity I said, "I shall never be moved." Lord, by Your favor You have made my mountain stand strong; You hid Your face, and I was troubled."*

Many people are like Samson –they are smart, intelligent, well connected. They think they could always get what they want, where and when they wanted it. So, there is no need for God or for prayers! How mistaken they are!

Proverbs 3:5-7 says:

> *"Trust in the Lord with all your heart, And lean not on your own understanding; In all your ways acknowledge Him, And He shall direct your paths. Do not be wise in your own eyes; Fear the Lord and depart from evil"*

In John 15:5-7, the Lord Jesus said:

> *"I am the vine, you are the branches. He who abides in Me, and I in him, bears much fruit; for without Me you can do nothing. If anyone does not abide in Me, he is cast out as a branch and is withered; and they gather them and throw them into the fire, and they are burned. If you abide in Me, and My words abide in you, you will ask what you desire, and it shall be done for you".*

A closer look at the above prayer of Samson reveals a few things: "O Lord God, remember me" was a desperate call to God by Samson asking God to please not forget him.

What could Samson be asking God to remember? It may be that he, Samson, realized that he was after all, an ordinary dust. There are many a man in leadership positions, their utterances and actions convey the impression that they are in charge. They think they are in control. The truth is that it is not what men say about them that matters but what God says. He is the all-seeing God, and He is the One who will do the final marking. Without God, all men are less than nothing!

Samson, without any doubt, must also have called upon God for mercy –that God should temper His judgment with mercy. Like the Prodigal son (in Luke 15:17-20), Samson must have come to realize that he had been taking God for granted - living in sin and expecting the grace of God to abound (Romans 6:1-2).

So, he prayed: 'Remember me, O God, please don't let Your mercy expire over me'.

Samson went on in his prayer: "Strengthen me, I pray, just this once". Here, Samson must have been saying "Lord, please give me another chance - just one more chance. I believe there are some people whom God is giving another chance. May be you are one of them, please don't waste it!

What are we to do so we don't fall into Samson's error and also end the way Samson ended?

The first is to know that God has a purpose for your life:
"Then the word of the LORD came to me, saying:"

> *"Before I formed you in the womb I knew you; Before you were born I sanctified you; I ordained you a prophet to the nations."... "For I know the thoughts that I think toward you, says the LORD, thoughts of peace and not of evil, to give you a future and a hope. ¹²Then you will call upon Me and go and pray to Me, and I will listen to you. ¹³And you will seek Me and find Me, when you search for Me with all your heart. ¹⁴I will be found by you, says the LORD, and I will bring you back from your captivity; I will gather you from all the nations and from all the places where I have driven you, says the LORD, and I will bring you to the place from which I cause you to be carried away captive".*
>
> **(Jeremiah 1:4-5; Jeremiah 29:11-14)**

Second, don't take God for granted. If you have been doing so, stop it today!:

> *"Then Peter opened his mouth and said: "In truth I perceive that God shows no partiality. ³⁵But in every nation whoever fears Him and works righteousness is accepted by Him."*
>
> **(Acts 10:34-35).**

Third, know that sin is a destiny destroyer. Hence stay far from sin - in fact flee from it. We are warned:

> *"Abstain from every form of evil.* ^{23}*Now may the God of peace Himself sanctify you completely; and may your whole spirit, soul, and body be preserved blameless at the coming of our Lord Jesus Christ.* ^{24}*He who calls you is faithful, who also will do it."*
>
> **(I Thessalonians 5:22-24).**

In Genesis 39:7-9, Joseph fled. He knew that the devil was after two critical things in his life—First, God's presence in and around him (Genesis 39:2-3,5,21-23); and second, the great destiny that God had for him. Thank God that Joseph ran for his life. At the end, he became great. Also, he could not be robbed of God's presence. At the end, his destiny could not be arrested (Genesis 45:8).

You may want to pray as follows:
- Father, thank You for Your Word. Thank You for speaking to me.
- Father, thank You for Your Master plan for my life. I know that I am not an accident of nature - You made me for a great purpose. I am a child of destiny.
- Please help me to fulfill my purpose in life.
- Anywhere I have been taking You for granted, please

have mercy upon me today.
- Every plan of the devil to cut short my life, Father, please destroy today.
- Father, whatever is in my life that the devil can use to destroy me, uproot today.
- Father let the work of all destiny robbers in my life end today.
- Father, separate me from anything and anyone who is out to take me from Your presence and take Your presence from me.

Perhaps you have never invited and received Jesus into your heart, please do so today. Your life is too precious, and eternity is too long for you to gamble with (Prov. 28:13; Rom 6:1-2; 23).

Please, pray this prayer loudly to Heaven:
"Lord Jesus, it is true and I acknowledge it that I am a sinner. I need Your forgiveness. I believe that You died in my place to pay the penalty for my sins, and that You rose from the dead. I turn from my sins, and ask You to have mercy on me. Please wash me in Your Blood. Lord Jesus, I receive You into my heart as my Saviour and Lord, Amen"
(Please see John 3:3-5; Acts 4:12; Proverbs 28:13; I John 1:5-9).

THE GOD
OF ALL POSSIBILITIES

3.1 The God of all possibilities

3.2 The Unchangeable Changer

3.3 Who is Like unto Thee, O Lord?

3.4 Let the Fire Fall!

3.5 A Miracle like a Dream

Chapter 3.1

The God of All Possibilities

⁹ *And so it was, when they had crossed over, that Elijah said to Elisha, "Ask! What may I do for you, before I am taken away from you?" Elisha said, "Please let a double portion of your spirit be upon me."* ¹⁰ *So he said, "You have asked a hard thing. Nevertheless, if you see me when I am taken from you, it shall be so for you; but if not, it shall not be so."* ¹¹ *Then it happened, as they continued on and talked, that suddenly a chariot of fire appeared with horses of fire, and separated the two of them; and Elijah went up by a whirlwind into heaven.* ¹² *And Elisha saw it, and he cried out, "My father, my father, the chariot of Israel and its horsemen!" So he saw him*

no more. And he took hold of his own clothes and tore them into two pieces. He took up also the mantle of Elijah that fell from him, and went back, and stood by the bank of Jordan; 14 And he took the mantle of Elijah that fell from him, and smote the waters, and said, Where is the LORD God of Elijah? and when he also had smitten the waters, they parted hither and thither: and Elisha went over"

(II Kings 2:9-14).

There are two main words in our subject matter for this chapter: GOD, and POSSIBILITIES.

About GOD, the Psalmist said:
"The fool has said in his heart, "There is no God." They are corrupt, They have done abominable works, There is none who does good."

(See also Romans 1:24-28).

A lot is worth knowing about God. For example, Who He is - His person and character attributes. Also worth knowing are His principles, His purpose or purposes, and the Master plan He has in mind for us as individuals. The knowledge of all these will help us to fulfil His purposes. Very crucial also, are His power, and His judgments, etc.

The word "POSSIBILITIES", among other things connotes the likelihood of a thing occurring or not occurring. It also means opportunities, alternatives or options. Possibilities can also be described as choices, a combination of factors, or forces that can determine the outcome of something.

When we talk about THE GOD OF ALL POSSIBILITIES, therefore, we are referring to the ONE who is Master and Lord over all things - both men, situations, circumstances, etc.

The God of all possibilities is also the One who is sovereign. It is HE who has the final say. When He says Yes, there is no one who can say No! (Please see Psalm 115:3; Lamentation 3:37; Revelation 3:7).

The God of all possibilities is the One who can reverse the irreversibles.

In addition, He is the One whom time, space and resources cannot hinder or limit from doing whatever He wants to.

Instances of the great acts of this God of all possibilities abound all around us. In the Bible, the Creation story as well as God's move among His people - the Israelites, are quite revealing. Such deeds range from mighty deliverances to divine interventions, and supernatural provisions. In the Church, from inception and throughout the Book of The Acts of the Apostles, as well as the Epistles, and even to the present day, the God of all possibilities has not stopped working miracles!(Please see Matthew 16:18-19; Acts 3:2-9;Acts 5:1-12; Acts 8:5-9; Acts 19:11-12).

When one comes to specific cases of God's move in Nations, church denominations, and in the individual lives of His children, one cannot but acknowledge the greatness of this awesome God. My personal life is full of evidences of the mighty moves of the God of all possibilities. From the time I came to know Him personally through to the present, space will not permit a full account of all He did and has been doing in all the places He sent us to in life and ministry. I have come to the conclusion that truly, the God of all possibilities has no limit.

In fact, what had made all the difference in every situation and place we went, or we had been to, is the presence, or absence of THE GOD OF ALL POSSIBILITIES!

That is why at times I laugh when I read the story of Naaman (II Kings 5:1-19). He had come to a man of God for help. When he was asked to go and bath seven (7) times in River Jordan, he flared up, and began to compare River Jordan with the rivers of Damascus. Thank God that before long, he came to realize that there are rivers and there were rivers, but the River Jordan was different!

In the same way, there are gods and there are gods, BUT there is ONLY one GOD OF ALL POSSIBILITIES. HE IS THE FATHER OF OUR LORD JESUS CHRIST. May that God visit you today in Jesus Name.

That takes us to our main Text (II Kings 2:9-14) - In brief, the Man of God, Elijah was about to be taken to Heaven. He felt it was a good time for him to reward his Servant who had been very faithful and diligent. So, he asked Elisha: *'What can I do for you before I am taken away from you'?* He was more or less giving Elisha an open Cheque and Elisha maximized the opportunity. By the time Elisha filled in what he wanted, Elijah realized that he had no resources enough to meet the request. So, he (Elijah) said,

> ***'You have asked a hard thing. Nevertheless, if you see me when I am taken from you, you will get what you asked for."***

Let us look at a few lessons from the story.

The first lesson here is that even though there are some things God can use Anointed men of God for in our lives, yet, they have their own limitations. There are many things they can never do for us (II Kings 4:27). The only ONE who is never limited is GOD Himself.

As we read in the passage, to show how limited he was, Prophet Elijah said to Elisha: *"What you have asked is hard."*

That takes us to the second lesson: In life, and as far as man is concerned, few things are really simple. Rather, many things are hard, some are even very hard. Not only that, some things are outrightly impossible.

The good news is that with our God, nothing is hard, and nothing is too hard.

In Genesis 18:13-14, the Bible said:
> **"And the Lord said to Abraham, "Why did Sarah laugh, saying, 'Shall I surely bear a child, since I am old?'**
> **¹⁴ Is anything too hard for the Lord? At the appointed**

time I will return to you, according to the time of life, and Sarah shall have a son".

There is another greater good news - it is in Jeremiah 32:17, 27:
Ah, Lord God! Behold, You have made the heavens and the earth by Your great power and outstretched arm. There is nothing too hard for You..........."*Behold, I am the Lord, the God of all flesh. Is there anything too hard for Me?"*

Luke 1:36-37 tell us:
"Now indeed, Elizabeth your relative has also conceived a son in her old age; and this is now the sixth month for her who was called barren. ³⁷For with God nothing will be impossible."

Many times when we have needs, we focus on human beings and/or human systems. May God help us to focus on Him and Him alone in Jesus Name. Why are we to, and must focus on God and Him alone? It is because human beings and the systems they created are all limited. ONLY GOD HAS NO LIMITATIONS. He is the Almighty. He is unlimited in power, in resources, in wisdom, in knowledge, in ability and readiness to help. May He surprise you for good today in Jesus Name.

Tell yourself: "MY CASE WILL NOT BE IMPOSSIBLE FOR GOD".

The third lesson from our Text is that even when things are hard, difficult, and seemingly impossible, somehow God still works out some solutions. Such situations, or problems could still be tackled, provided certain conditions are met. For example, if there is <u>Genuine Repentance</u>.

The Bible says;
> *"He who covers his sins will not prosper, But whoever confesses and forsakes them will have mercy"*
> **(Please see Proverbs 28:13; Isaiah 55:6-7).**

By genuine repentance we mean a true and ready heart to change our ways for the better. This covers confession of, and seeking forgiveness from all intentional and unintentional sins.

It is important too, to confess our sin of not being sensitive enough to God's voice. As a Missionary, way back in 1996, the Lord opened a door to start a new Branch of our denomination (The RCCG) in the UK, specifically in the Swiss Cottage, North London. On one Sunday, I got to the Community Hall we were using for our Sunday worship services, and the key to the Hall allocated to us was not in the place where I normally picked it from. Meanwhile, worshippers were already gathering and anxious to enter the Hall. In desperation, I asked God for mercy. Of course, I first acknowledged that God knew everything in advance and hence He knew wherever the key to the Hall was. I also repented for my not being sensitive enough to hear Him give me an advance information. I asked God for divine intervention and direction. To my amazement, I heard God telling me to pick any key on the Board and go to the main door to the Hall. I obeyed. The door opened, and the Service went very well. It was about 5.00 pm later that day that we knew what had happened: the leader of the group that used the Hall the previous night had forgotten to drop the key in the Box Room. He left with the key and didn't realize his mistake until 3:30 pm on that Sunday! Thank God for the God of all possibilities, He stepped in. May God help us to always be sensitive to His leading in Jesus Name.

Also, if there is a <u>Restitution</u> to make, don't hesitate or procrastinate:

> *" Then Zacchaeus stood and said to the Lord, "Look, Lord, I give half of my goods to the poor; and if I have taken anything from anyone by false accusation, I restore fourfold."*
> *⁹And Jesus said to him, "Today salvation has come to this house, because he also is a son of Abraham; ¹⁰for*

the Son of Man has come to seek and to save that which was lost."

(Luke 19:8-10)

In addition, solutions come when we bring GOD into the equation - the God with whom nothing is impossible.

In I Samuel 1:9-20 is the story of Hannah. She went to Shiloh and God visited her. Verses 19-20 tell us:

"Then they rose early in the morning and worshiped before the Lord, and returned and came to their house at Ramah. And Elkanah knew Hannah his wife, and the Lord remembered her. ²⁰ So it came to pass in the process of time that Hannah conceived and bore a son, and called his name Samuel, saying, "Because I have asked for him from the Lord."

May be you are a woman, or you are a man, and your wife is in Hannah's situation, may the Word of the Lord reach you now in Jesus Name. May the Lord do unto you what He did for Hannah. May He put a permanent end to your waiting and weeping in Jesus Name. May you begin to prepare for your own Samuel too in Jesus Name. Verse 19 of the above quoted passage said: *"Elkannah knew his wife* (as at other times)…*'and the LORD remembered her"*. You and your wife or husband may have been knowing each other for some time. This season, the LORD will remember you in Jesus Name!

I pray today, that this season, God will bring forth several Samuels in as many homes as have need for it, in Jesus Name.

There was a particular condition to be met for Elisha to have what he requested: *"If you see me when I am taken from you"..*

There is something to note here: It was a certainty that Elijah was going to be taken away that day– both of them (Elijah and Elisha) knew it well. Even the Sons of the Prophets everywhere, knew it. This brings us to the fourth lesson:
Each day is made up of 24 Hours. It is one thing to know the day that something is meant to happen, but it is another thing entirely to know the Hour and moment for it to happen. Many a pregnant woman knew the expected delivery dates (EDD) of the babies in their womb. However, it is only the Almighty God who knows the hour and moment of safe delivery! When your day of miracle comes, may you not miss the hour and moment in Jesus Name.

Not only that, it is also another thing to be prepared and ready for the thing.

In Matthew 24:3, the Disciples had asked Jesus some hard questions:

> *"Tell us, when shall these things be? And what shall be the sign of Thy coming, and the end of the world?"*

After giving them several signs, the Lord Jesus told them in Verse 36:

> *"But of the Day and Hour knoweth no man, no, not the angels of Heaven, but my Father only".*

To further illustrate His point, in Matthew 25:1-13, our Lord then gave the parable of the Ten Virgins: All the Ten of them knew the Day, BUT ONLY five were wise enough to know and to prepare for the Hour! May God make me and you, Dear Reader, wise to the end in Jesus Name. May God help us to watch, pray, and prepare in Jesus Name, AMEN!

Talking about watching, one may ask: what is there to watch, and probably, how do we watch? First, everyone is to watch over his or her own life. In Corinthians 9:27; I Peter 5:8-9, we read:

> *"But I discipline my body and bring it into subjection, lest, when I have preached to others, I myself should become disqualified.".*
> *"Be sober, be vigilant; because your adversary the devil walks about like a roaring lion, seeking whom*

he may devour. Resist him, steadfast in the faith, knowing that the same sufferings are experienced by your brotherhood in the world."

We are to be on guard 24/7 - so we can finish well.

We are to live a holy life. We are not to joke with the issue of Holiness (please see I Peter 1:15-16; Hebrews 12:14).

Furthermore, we are to let the Word of God dwell richly in us. Whenever we read or hear the Word of God, we should let the word 'be to us and for us'. This is the key to a godly and holy living (please see Psalm 119: 11; Colossians 3:16; James 1: 22-26).

Finally, we are to do away with every frivolity, carnality, and vanity. (Psalm 1:1-3; II Corinthians 6:14-18, 7:1).

The <u>fifth lesson</u> (from our main Text), has to do with the issue of focus.

When the Chariot of fire, the Horses of fire, and the whirlwind came, Elisha would have had a singular focus –seeing Elijah, his master departing. Why is this so? – Because he (Elisha), had been told: "IF YOU SEE ME WHEN I AM TAKEN FROM YOU, THEN YOU CAN HAVE WHAT YOU ASKED FOR! – Elisha knew that his own life and destiny depended on seeing Elijah when he was being taken away.

Who and where are we to focus upon in these end times?: We are to focus on JESUS and HEAVEN! (See Heberews 12:2-3; Colossians 3:1-3).

Even for your miracles and whatever your needs, right now, - Who are you to focus upon? JESUS!
It is time for prayers:
- Father, thank You for loving me, and sending Your Word to me. Thank You for Your Word that has come to me and for me.
- Father, I know that nothing is hard or difficult for You, please surprise me today, and right now.
- Father, You are the God of all possibilities: please lift me up far beyond my expectations.
- Father, let today be my day, and this Hour/moment, my Hour and Moment for divine visitation.
- Father, help me to be watchful - don't let me miss my day/hour of Visitation.
- Father, that <u>very</u> help that I need, please send right now!

Perhaps you are yet to receive Jesus as your personal Saviour and Lord. The Bible says in Proverbs 28:13; Isaiah 55:6-7:

> *"He <u>who</u> covers his sins will not prosper, But <u>whoever</u> confesses and forsakes them will have mercy....Seek the Lord while He may be found, Call upon Him while He is near. Let the wicked forsake his way, And the unrighteous man his thoughts; Let him return to the Lord, And He will have mercy on him; And to our God, He will abundantly pardon"*

If you know that you need to get right with God, confess your sins to Him right where you are, then invite Jesus into your heart. Ask Him for mercy and forgiveness. I John 1:7-9 declares:

> *"But if we walk in the light as He is in the light, we have fellowship with one another, and the blood of Jesus Christ His Son cleanses us from all sin. If we say that we have no sin, we deceive ourselves, and the truth is not in us. If we confess our sins, He is faithful and just to forgive us our sins and to cleanse us from all unrighteousness."*

May be you are a Backslider, and what you need is restoration, Talk to God, ask Him to forgive and restore you.

It may be that all you need for your miracles to reach you now is restitution – to undo the evils you have done in the past. Please go ahead and ask God for the grace and wisdom to do it.

- May be you can prayerfully sing this popular Hymn/song with me:

> *"Pass me not, O Gentle Saviour, hear my humble cry,*
> *While on others Thou art calling, Do not pass me by.*
> *Saviour, Saviour hear my humble cry, Whilst on others Thou art calling, Do not pass me by!"*

(You can also call Him: *Gentle Healer, Gentle Deliverer, Destiny Helper, etc*).

I pray for you, that:
- God will put an end to every vain labour in your life, and He will replace all your labour with His Favour.
- all enemies and relations who pretend to be friends, will be exposed and incapacitated in Jesus Name.
- God will open your eyes to see your destiny helpers (especially that life partner).
- every contrary wind or storm will be silenced.
- in spite of what happened to you recently, your confidence and courage in yourself, and in God will be restored.
- the good news you have been believing God for, will come this week, in Jesus Name.

Chapter 3.2

The Unchangeable Changer

"For I am the Lord, I do not change; Therefore you are not consumed, O sons of Jacob."...
"Thus says the Lord, your Redeemer, The Holy One of Israel: "For your sake I will send to Babylon, And bring them all down as fugitives— The Chaldeans, who rejoice in their ships. I am the Lord, your Holy One, The Creator of Israel, your King." Thus says the Lord, who makes a way in the sea And a path through the mighty waters, Who brings forth the chariot and horse, The army and the power (They shall lie down together, they shall not rise; They are extinguished, they are quenched like a wick): "Do not remember the former things, Nor consider the things of old. Behold,

I will do a new thing, Now it shall spring forth; Shall you not know it? I will even make a road in the wilderness And rivers in the desert."

(Mal 3:6; Isa 43:14-19).

When we say that something or someone is UNCHANGEABLE, it means that thing or person remains the same. It also means that the thing or person cannot and will not change no matter the pressure applied either from within or from outside. Another word for 'UNCHANGEABLE' is 'CONSTANT'. Anything that does not or cannot change must be constant!

We are living in a world of change. The reason is simple: God created this earth with an inherent ability for change. Ecclesiastics 3:1-8 says:

> *"To everything there is a season, A time for every purpose under heaven: A time to be born, And a time to die; A time to plant, And a time to pluck what is planted; A time to kill, And a time to heal; A time to break down, And a time to build up; A time to weep, And a time to laugh; A time to mourn, And a time to dance; A time to cast away stones, And a time to gather stones; A time to embrace, And a time to refrain from embracing; A time to gain, And a time to*

lose; A time to keep, And a time to throw away; A time to tear, And a time to sew; A time to keep silence, And a time to speak; A time to love, And a time to hate; A time of war, And a time of peace."

The Bible makes it clear here - "*To everything there is a season, A time for every purpose under heaven*" , this is purely talking about CHANGE! when one season gives way to another, It is a change. Hence, we have a time to be born and a time to die, a time to laugh, and a time to weep, we have day and also the night. There is seed-time, and harvest time, etc.

Perhaps central to many, if not most changes is human beings. We change, and we also change things. Moreover, things also change us! As men, we do change a lot. We change in size and in appearances. Some people change in their values-what they called bad before is no more bad or evil, and what they used to call good in the past is no more good!

Because we change in values, our lifestyle and relationships too often change.

Not only do we change, things change us. For example, position, money, wealth, women, wrong philosophies, religion, etc, change our perception.

Very importantly, some people change when hardship, suffering, lack and betrayal set in.

As an agent of change, man can change a thick jungle into city. A man filled with the Holy Spirit and a godly vision, can turn millions of sinners into Christ's followers, etc. The other side is also true. A man that is possessed with an evil, wicked and a blood-thirsty spirit can turn a few men (soldiers or civilians) into murderers of thousands if not millions of innocent souls!

Other things that change and also do cause changes are government, technology, etc.

Perhaps the greatest change that man has effected in the last 100 years, is in the area of Science & Technology. Computer and digital technology has turned the world into a global village! All these are not without its costs

THE ONLY ONE who does not and can never change is <u>God</u>. In Malachi 3:6, this God said:
> *"For I am the* LORD, *I do not change; Therefore you are not consumed, O sons of Jacob."*

The truth that God does not change (and cannot change), is a very important attribute of God.

The Bible assures us that Jesus too does not change:
> *"Jesus Christ is the same yesterday, today, and forever."*
>
> (Hebrews 13:8).

There is a very important question that often agitate many a heart of men. They ask: WHY WILL GOD NOT CHANGE, irrespective of whatever happens? I can not claim to know too! However, I perceive it may be because of us human beings- especially because of those of us who are His children who are genuinely saved. Imagine, for a moment the possibility as well as the implication of God just changing a little (and for a very brief period)!

For e.g, if He were to change in His personality or character. One of the serious implications of this is that HIS WORD (the Bible), will no more be reliable. It also means that we can no more depend upon His promises. That alone, has a lot of implications for the entire Universe. In Hebrews 1:1-3, we read:

> *"God, who at various times and in various ways spoke in time past to the fathers by the prophets, ²has in these last days spoken to us by His Son, whom He has appointed heir of all things, through whom also He made the worlds; ³who being the brightness of His glory and the express image of His person, and upholding all things by the word of His power, when*

He had by Himself purged our sins, sat down at the right hand of the Majesty on high,"

THANK GOD THAT HE DOES NOT CHANGE! HIS WORD IS RELIABLE. Whatever God has said in His Word, He will surely do. Please see: Isaiah 1:19; Isaiah 3:10; Isaiah 1:20; Isaiah 3:11; Proverbs 28: 13; I John 1:5-9; Psalm 1:1-3; etc.

It is interesting to note that this great and UNCHANGEABLE GOD is the greatest Changer! He is the One who has the ultimate power to change all and anything. He is the ALMIGHTY. HE is also Sovereign and Supreme (Please see Psalm 115:3; Lamentation 3:37).

In Isaiah 43:18-19, He said:

"Do not remember the former things, Nor consider the things of old. Behold, I will do a new thing, Now it shall spring forth; Shall you not know it? I will even make a road in the wilderness And rivers in the desert."

What are the things God can change? Let's look at just three: First, He can change Seasons and times.

Daniel 2:19-22 tell us that God has power to change seasons and times.

Second, the unchangeable God can also change Circumstances and Situations. For example, He can change sickness to health (please see Psalm 107: 20; John 5:1-9). He can change scarcity to plenty or abundance (I Kings 17:8-16). He can change failure to success (Luke 5:1-9). He can change hardships and famine, etc for individuals and Nations. He can change barrenness to fruitfulness (I Samuel 2:5, 21). He can change disappointment to appointment (please see Genesis 37: 5-9; Genesis 41: 14, 37-41). He can change death to life (Ezekiel 33:11; John 11:38-44). He can make the last to become No 1 - I Samuel 16:1-13).

Thirdly, God can change Names and destinies - both for individuals and for Nations.

On some occasions in the Bible, God had to change the names of some people before they could prosper and fulfil their destinies. Among such people are Abraham and his wife (see Genesis 17:4-16; Genesis 32:24-29).

I don't know what situations you may be in or the challenges you may be facing, I have good news for you: THE UNCHANGEABLE CHANGER is close to you. I pray that He will intervene in your case this day in Jesus Name, Amen. For God's power to affect you positively and for good, you must position yourself in a way that will make it easy for Him to help you. In Matthew 11:28-30, the Lord Jesus said:

> *"Come to Me, all you who labor and are heavy laden, and I will give you rest. Take My yoke upon you and learn from Me, for I am gentle and lowly in heart, and you will find rest for your souls. For My yoke is easy and My burden is light."*

What HE is saying here to you is: 'Come, let Me change you for good, Let Me forgive you your sins, and give you a New Beginning.

Dear Reader, if you are not very sure of your relationship with Jesus Christ, you can be sure from today. All you need is to confess your sins to Him where you are. Ask Him to forgive you and cleanse you with His precious BLOOD. Then invite Him into your heart. Then ask Him to give you the power to live a life that pleases Him.

Call upon God also, and ask Him to take over every battle you are facing (or that is facing you). Ask Him to give you all-around victory (especially spiritually, maritally, financially, mentally, etc).

Chapter 3.3

"Who is Like Unto Thee, O Lord?"

"The enemy said, I will pursue, I will overtake, I will divide the spoil; My desire shall be satisfied upon them; I will draw my sword, my hand shall destroy them. Thou didst blow with thy wind, the sea covered them: They sank as lead in the mighty waters. Who is like unto thee, O Jehovah, among the gods? Who is like thee, glorious in holiness, Fearful in praises, doing wonders?
Thou in thy loving kindness hast led the people that thou hast redeemed: Thou hast guided them in thy strength to thy holy habitation."

- (Exodus 15:9-12)

The Question: "WHO IS LIKE UNTO THEE, O LORD?", is our focus in this Chapter. The crucial Question was asked by the Israelites. They were asking - "O Lord, who can we compare You with?" A similar question had been asked by God Himself in Isaiah 40:18, 25:

> *"The image, a workman hath cast it, and the goldsmith overlayeth it with gold, and casteth for it silver chains. To whom then will ye liken me, that I should be equal to him? saith the Holy One."*

The Question in Exodus 15:11, was provoked by about four things.

First, by the hopelessness of the situation facing the Israelites, and the desperation of the people - this made them to cry to Moses. At times we become desperate and look unto men - we forget that it is only God who can help us. Men can come to our rescue but that will happen ONLY and ONLY IF GOD moves them to do so. Thank God that here, He showed up for His people. May He show up for you at your time of need in Jesus Name.

Perhaps as you are reading this book, you are currently facing some seemingly hopeless situations. I pray that before this day is over, you will hear good news in Jesus Name.

Second, the Question was provoked by what God did for His people. God had just made a way where there was none. He also ensured that the enemies who would not let His people enjoy their freedom and liberty were wiped out completely. The Bible said the Lord troubled the chariots, the horses, and the horsemen of Pharaoh. Today, may God make ways for you where there had been none in Jesus Name. I pray too that God will trouble all your troublers in Jesus Name.

In case it appears that your destiny is under threat, today, God will give you a new song in Jesus Name.

The third thing that provoked the Question is the way God did what He did at the crossing of the Red Sea: God partnered with Moses. God told him to stretch forth his hand over the Sea, then God caused an East wind to blow.

To perform most miracles, God has His own side. We as human beings have our part too. We can not do what He alone can do. Of course, He can not, and will not do what He has given us the wherewithal to do. Today, God is still seeking men to partner with. May He help us to do our part in Jesus Name.

The final thing that provoked that Question we are looking at is what God used in performing the miracle. God used the wind.

God is the Maker and Controller of all - men, Kings, air, winds, sea, waters, etc.

Whatever God must use to meet your needs or solve your problems - whether human agents, the elements, etc, may He go ahead and do so today in Jesus Name.

Let us look at some possible answers to this great Question: "WHO IS LIKE UNTO THEE O LORD?"

The first answer is that THERE IS NO ONE LIKE UNTO OUR GOD: There is a song that says: "God alone is God, and God is God alone".

Even though over the ages men had endeavoured to fill the space God created for Himself in every man's heart with several other things, yet nothing can ever truly fill that space. All the things that had become idols and gods, and which had displaced or replaced God in the heart of men CAN NEVER bring peace, joy or satisfaction. Many had turned to money, position, power, fame, or whatever, name it - even Ministry!

Solomon described as the wisest man that ever lived on this planet earth told us all he did. A Bible Commentator said "While on the one hand, Job could not find meaning in his sufferings,

Solomon, on the other hand could not find meaning in all his accomplishments and joy." No wonder, Solomon admonished in Ecclesiastics 12:13-14:

> *"Let us hear the conclusion of the whole matter: Fear God and keep His commandments, For this is man's all. ¹⁴ For God will bring every work into judgment, Including every secret thing, Whether good or evil."*

WHO THEN IS OUR GOD?

Our Text described Him as "glorious in holiness". Our God is holy. Holiness is His trademark. He demands that all His children be holy. He also demands holiness from all His Ministers (Lev 19:1-2; I Peter 1:15-16; II Tim 2:19).

In fact, the higher God takes a person in His Service, the more He will demand that he or she moves to a higher degree of holiness. At a new and higher level of Service or calling, you will discover that there are some things you will not be able to do, some places you won't be able to go, and some people you won't be able to relate with. There may even be some dresses you may not be able to wear again!

Not only is God holy, He is glorious in holiness. His holiness is radiant, and it also bestows glory which the enemy can not approach. Neither can they contest or contend with it. It was such glory that got reflected on Moses after he had been on the mountain in God's presence for forty days.

God is also fearful in praises. The Bible said a lot about God and praises. Our God loves praises, and He deserves praises. God also demands praises, and expects praises. He dwells in the praises of His people, and God uses praises as a weapon of warfare (See II Chronicles 20:12- 27; Acts 16:25-31; Psalm 149:1-9).

God specifically warned against stealing His praise.

Finally, God rewards praises. This may probably be the main reason why David excelled in all he did in life. He did not allow any new success or promotion to rob him of praising God. It is a wise thing to refuse to let anything or anyone to prevent you from praising God, no matter how big, how rich or how successful you become. Also, whatever God does through you, it is wise to learn to return ALL the glory and praise to Him.

God is a wonder working God. He is the only God who does true Wonders. He does things that only He alone can explain the why, and how of. There are several stories in the Bible that make me wonder at God - His ways, His acts, His wisdom, His timing, etc. Our God is Sovereign. For example, the crossing of the Red Sea. Also, the story of Hannah - her long barrenness (and how she later became the mother of six children – all from the same womb)!

Where do you and I come into all these?
-   It is critical to know your God very well. You must know Him in person. You must know His character, His ways and principles In Psalm 103:7, we read:

> ***"He made known His ways to Moses, His acts to the children of Israel."***

-   We must also know God's purpose and plan

We must refrain from using the balance wheel of another man's wrist watch to run our own!

-   We must fear God and obey Him. We must not take God for granted. If for any reason you have been taking Him for granted, stop it today! (See Acts 10:34-35)
-   We are to focus on fulfilling His plans for our lives. There is no doubt that there will be challenges.

Both people and situations will be there to distract, discourage and divert our attention, but we are to be resolute on standing upon God's Word (Hebrews 12:1-3).

These prayer points will surely be good for you:

* Father, I know there is no one You can be compared with. On a daily basis, please show me Your greatness.
* Father, as You made a way in the Red Sea, please make a way for me.
* Father, as You drowned all the enemies who pursued Your children into the Red Sea, Father, do the same to all who would not want me to reach my goal.
* Father, please teach me to praise You. Help me to always remember to give You the praise that is due to Your Name.
* Father, You are the God of Wonders, please perform wonders in my life, and use me to perform wonders.

Chapter 3.4

Let Fire Fall!

"And it came to pass, at the time of the offering of the evening sacrifice, that Elijah the prophet came near and said, "Lord God of Abraham, Isaac, and Israel, let it be known this day that You are God in Israel and I am Your servant, and that I have done all these things at Your word. Hear me, O Lord, hear me, that this people may know that You are the Lord God, and that You have turned their hearts back to You again."
Then <u>the fire of the Lord fell and consumed</u> the burnt sacrifice, and the wood and the stones and the dust, and it licked up the water that was in the trench. Now when all the people saw it, they <u>fell on</u>

their faces; and they said, "*The Lord, He is God! The Lord, He is God!.*"

(I Kings 18:36-39).

In the Bible, there are many cases of fire falling from Heaven - physically or in other forms. (Please see Exodus 3:1-7; Exodus 19:1-20; I Kings 18; II Kings 1:7-14; Acts 2:1-4).

Hence the need for us to know more about this important object or substance called Fire.

First, fire has some characteristics. For example, fire is an indiscriminate consumer! It deals with anything in its way, except there is a divine restraint.

Fire also transforms and brings out the potentials in whatever it touches -be it oil, water, man, or other natural mineral resources like petrol, iron, gold, diamond, etc.

Second, fire has some association or link with God. For instance, in Hebrews 12:28-29, God the Father is described as the consuming fire!

"*[28] Therefore, since we are receiving a kingdom which cannot be shaken, let us have grace, by which we*

[28]may serve God acceptably with reverence and godly fear. [29]For our God is a consuming fire."

Also, in Matthew 3:11, God the Son (our Lord Jesus Christ, is described as the Baptizer with the Holy Ghost and with Fire:
"I indeed baptize you with water unto repentance, but He who is coming after me is mightier than I, whose sandals I am not worthy to carry. He will baptize you with the Holy Spirit and fire."

At Pentecost, the Holy Spirit came as the Fire from Heaven (please see Acts 2:1-4).

What are all these saying to us? I believe they are warning us to be careful how we relate with or handle fire. Be careful how you relate with God. Do not take Him for granted. Do not play games with God! If you do, you may not go scot free!

Third, physically when Fire is at work, several things can happen. For example, impurities are burnt off - it is similar to what takes place in refineries. The same is true in the spiritual. In Acts 2: 1-4, all the impurities in the lives of the Disciples, especially Peter, were burnt off by the fire of the Holy Spirit. One of those impurities was fear or timidity.

When fire falls, bondages and yokes are destroyed - both physically and spiritually. In Acts 16:25-31, we see this happen in the lives of Paul and Silas.

Another thing that can happen when the fire of God falls is that ways open –(Exodus 14:14-16).

Very importantly too, when fire falls, power is transferred. One of the first effects of the Pentecost experience was the miracle that happened to the lame man at the Beautiful Gate (See Acts 3:2-9). The power in the hands of Peter and John flowed into the body of the lame man, and his ankle bones received life.

When fire falls, there is a transformation and hidden potentials are brought out, which leads to more usefulness.

When fire is applied to water and oil, and they get heated to a certain temperature, they can do more than when at normal room temperature.

Every human being needs the Fire of God to transform us and help release our potentials. Some people still prefer to be asking for help when they should be helping others. Some people prefer to remain tenants when they should be landlords. Also, some people prefer to sit down in churches when they should be pastors and teachers in new Parishes. Today, may the fire of God fall, and cause a release in Jesus Name.

When fire falls, there is a translation. This is a sign that the one whom the Fire fell for, has finished well. The day Elijah was to be taken to Heaven by a whirlwind, the first thing that came was the chariots and horses of Fire.

When the fire falls, Unrepentant sinners and the wicked are judged. A rebellious clique like Korah, Datha and Abiram, as well as compulsive liars and blackmailers like Gehazi and Ananias with his wife Saphira, won't go scot free (Please see Num 16:1-33; II Kings 5:19-27; Acts 12:1-12).

In our opening text, we see four things that preceded the arrival of God's fire: There was a preparation for the Fire. Prophet Elijah first repaired the altar that had broken down. In the same way, everything that separated us from God and His holy standard must be dealt with. Anything of self-including pride, arrogance, self- righteousness, hypocrisy, unforgiving spirit, and the spiritual blindness that did not let you see the big picture, etc must be uprooted.

There was a recognition of the Lord's timing. Many of us often do things that appear we have gone ahead of God. At other times, we also take steps that show we lag, far behind Him. Hence the need to be conscious of God's timing.

There was also prayers. Elijah called upon God (See James 5:16-18). There are Prayers and there are Prayers. When, instead of repenting and asking God for mercy, a man, a family, a church, or a Nation is praying for prosperity, promotion and breakthrough, it is simply a waste of time. It means such a man, family, church, or Nation does not understand God or His principles (Romans 6:1-2; Prov 28:13-14)..

Finally, the arrival of the Fire itself. On this particular occasion, when the fire of God fell, there were creative and restorative miracles. Also, there was the ultimate return and restoration of God's people to Him. Finally, God executed judgment on all His enemies!

> *Who are you attracting to your church, and how are you attracting them? If you use carnal means to attract people to church, it is only carnal people you will have, and you will need more carnal means to retain them! (Please see Romans 8:5-9; John 14:6).*

In conclusion, in Matthew 13:33, we read:
> *Another parable He spoke to them: "The kingdom of heaven is like leaven, which a woman took and hid in*

three measures of meal till it was all leavened." (KJV)
NLT: Jesus also used this illustration: "The Kingdom of Heaven is like the yeast a woman used in making bread. Even though she put only a little yeast in three measures of flour, it permeated every part of the dough."

This story or parable is about a woman baker. She hid a little yeast in a loaf and the yeast permeated the whole loaf. How did it happen or what made it possible? It was because some Fire was applied. The application or introduction of Fire led to several things. When the Fire of the Holy Spirit permeates a man, several things will also happen (as we have enumerated above).

It's time to pray:
- Father, let the Fire fall - Your Fire - the Fire of the Holy Ghost. Let that fire permeate my whole being.
- Father, let my own fire fall so that I too can permeate my land and my generation.
- Father, purify me, transform me, and let me realize my potentials.
- Father, let Your Fire fall to surround and defend me.
- Father, let every bitter water in my life be made sweet.
- Father, open a new chapter for me, and put an end to all age-long health problems in my family.

- Father, right now please manifest Your glory in my life, and let all who have written me off receive divine surprises.
- Father, everywhere men have marked me wrong, please mark me right, today.

Chapter 3.5

A Miracle Like A Dream!

"1 When the LORD turned again the captivity of Zion, we were like them that dream. 2 Then was our mouth filled with laughter, and our tongue with singing: then said they among the heathen, The LORD hath done great things for them. 3 The LORD hath done great things for us; whereof we are glad. 4 Turn again our captivity, O LORD, as the streams in the south. 5 They that sow in tears shall reap in joy. 6 He that goeth forth and weepeth, bearing precious seed, shall doubtless come again with rejoicing, bringing his sheaves with him."

(Psalm 126:1-6).

The Psalm quoted above says a lot about God - especially, His Almightiness and that when God speaks, He will definitely do whatever He says (Numbers 23:19; Hebrews 13:13-18).

In this Chapter, we shall concentrate on Vs 1-2:
> *"1 When the LORD turned again the captivity of Zion, we were like them that dream. 2 Then was our mouth filled with laughter, and our tongue with singing: then said they among the heathen, The LORD hath done great things for them."*

In Verse 1 of the passage, we read:
> ***"When the LORD turned again the captivity of Zion"***.

I want to invite our attention to the word 'when'. The Bible says here "WHEN" not "IF". This implies that God had already done it. Also, it is to be noted that when our God speaks, it is settled. It's only a matter of time, IT MUST SURELY COME TO PASS. In Isaiah 40:8; and Psalm 119:89, we read:
> *"The grass withers, the flower fades, But the word of our God stands forever."..."Forever, O LORD, Your word is settled in heaven"*.

It is important to point out that the very fact that the Word of God is settled and would surely come to pass, is not just in the area of Blessings and Breakthroughs, but also in all other areas of life! (Please find time to look at the following Scriptures: Isaiah 1:19-20; Isaiah 3:10-11; Luke 6:38; Proverbs 3:9-10; Proverbs 11:21,23; Proverbs 28:13).

Second, and still in Vs1, the passage continued: "*The Lord turned again the captivity of Zion (I.e, God brought back their blessing)* IT WAS THE LORD WHO DID IT, NOT MAN! It was the Lord's doing, not their wisdom. In fact, on their part, the people of Israel had already lost every hope. What is this telling us?

By this, we realize that there is no hopeless situation with God. Also, whenever God performs a miracle in our lives, we should learn to give Him all the glory and praise (Isaiah 42:8).

Today, every hopeless situation in your life will receive Divine intervention in Jesus Name. What God alone can do in all areas of your life, He will do it in Jesus Name.

In Judges 7:1-2, God had to cut down the army of Gideon - from 32,000 soldiers to just 300! This is to prevent the Israelites from thinking that it was by their strength, wisdom and number that they won the battle.

The word 'Captivity' has been defined as the state of being kept in a place (such as prison or cage), and not being able to leave or be free. Acaptive is someone who had been captured and kept in prison or in a cage.

He is a person held under the control of another, even though he may have the appearance of independence. We have some classical examples in the Bible. These include Samson. In Judges 16:18-21, we read:

"When Delilah saw that he had told her all his heart, she sent and called for the lords of the Philistines, saying, "Come up once more, for he has told me all his heart." So the lords of the Philistines came up to herand brought the money in their hand.

[19] Then shelulled him to sleep on her knees, and called for a man and had him shave off the seven locks of his head. Then she began to torment him, and his strength left him. [20] And she said, "The Philistines are upon you, Samson!" So he awoke from his sleep, and said, "I will go out as before, at other times, and shake myself free!" But he did not know that the LORD had departed from him".

> *²¹Then the Philistines took him and put out his eyes, and brought him down to Gaza. They bound him with bronze fetters, and he became a grinder in the prison".*

King Ahab was another person who became a captive. Ahab had a terrible wife called Jezebel. In our book 'the First Voice', a whole chapter was devoted to underscoring the impact this woman had on the destiny of Ahab.

Nebuchadnezzar (the Babylonian king) was another captive. Pride made him obsessed with his achievement. For a whole year, in spite of warnings from God, he kept on boasting. God eventually jolted his brain a little, and for seven good years, he was in the bush as an animal until he came to his senses! One can go on and on. Perhaps you too are under the bondage of some forces that are compelling you to do some things or go into some activities that are inimical to your welfare, may the mighty Hand of the Almighty reach you in Jesus Name.

Today, in whatever way you may have been held captive, the Mighty Hand of God shall reach you and bring you total and permanent deliverance in Jesus Name.

How do people get captured or end up in captivity? This can happen in several ways.

First, a person can be born into captivity. For instance, all the children born to the Israelites while in Egypt, were born into captivity.

I once heard the story of a woman who was jailed for a crime but was later found to be pregnant. She gave birth to a baby boy who began to grow up in the premises of the prison. He went to school and made friends. He lived many years inside the prison compound. One day, the State Governor visited the prison and gave the mother of this boy amnesty. The boy's mother told her son "We are now free to go home!". The boy looked bewildered and asked his mother: "Going home, which home? This is home!"

Second, a person can be sold into captivity. The Brothers of Joseph conspired against Him and had him sold to a slave trader, who in turn, also sold him to Potiphar, an Egyptian captain of Guards. (Gen 40:14-15)

Third, a person can walk into captivity. Often, this happens through wrong desires, inordinate ambition, love of money, love of position and power, etc.

Finally, someone can be trapped and get into captivity through deception, evil covenant and so on.

It does not matter how a person got into captivity, or for how long he or she may have been in captivity, there is a good news - it is possible to come out of captivity!

This leads us to another crucial Question: Who can bring out of captivity? It is God, and Him alone who can bring out of captivity. How then does He do it? HE does it through His Son – the Lord JESUS! (See Matthew 11:28-31; John 8:32, 36).

However, for God to do so, we must cooperate with Him. We do this through repentance. We must repent of all our sins, and prepare to come out and be free!

Twice, in the Bible, we see Israel as a Nation gone into captivity – first in Egypt, and later in Babylon.

How did they get into captivity in Egypt? It began with a search for food. There was a severe famine in the land. Then the news came that there was plenty of food in Egypt. So, Jacob sent ten of his twelve sons to go and buy corn. Meanwhile, God had divinely sent Joseph ahead of them. Later Joseph made himself known to his Brothers. He asked them if his father was still alive.

Eventually, Jacob and sixty-six members of his family migrated into Egypt. They started procreating, and as time went on, they virtually outnumbered the Egyptians. Joseph and all the Elders passed away. Also a new King that knew not Joseph started ruling in Egypt. He feared that if any war should break out, Israel might support the enemies. So he came up with a plan to start eliminating new Israeli babies. This was the environment into which Moses was born (Genesis Chapters 41-47; 46:1-4, 26-27). Every child born in Egypt was automatically born into captivity!

Israel, because of her sin was exiled to Babylon. They had failed to heed God's warning to repent (II Chronicles 36:1-16, 17-21). They spent seventy long years in serious bondage.

Now, and very often, we look up to God for some divine intervention. When the miracle does not come, we tend to give up. May I give you a candid admonition: DON'T GIVE UP! Miracles still happen. Miracles still happen like a dream! In our main Text, the Israelites exclaimed:

> *"When the LORD turned again the captivity of Zion, we were like them that dream."*

Before this divine intervention took place, God's people had been in bondage and captivity in Babylon for nearly Seventy

Years. The enemy had taunted and mocked them times without number. In Psalm 137:1-4, we read:

> *"By the rivers of Babylon, There we sat down, yea, we wept When we remembered Zion. ²We hung our harps Upon the willows in the midst of it. ³For there those who carried us away captive asked of us a song, And those who plundered us requested mirth, Saying, "Sing us one of the songs of Zion!"⁴How shall we sing the LORD's song In a foreign land?"*

It had appeared that God's promise to bring them out and return them back to their homeland was never going to materialize again. Thank God that when He speaks, He will always honour His word. (Numbers 23:19). May God visit you today, (and me too), and uproot sickness and disease. May He also put an end to pains and sorrow in your life. May He touch your finances, and turn your lack or scarcity into abundance. I pray that the promotion you are believing God for, will come like a dream!

In Genesis 41, we find an interesting story: A young man named Joseph had been in Prison for an offense he did not commit. Someone met him there, and he thought help had come. He told the man the story of his life, and asked him to please remember him, but the man completely forgot all about Joseph. Two years went by. Then one morning, God remembered Joseph, and like a dream, his freedom came. You may be in Joseph's shoes, it may appear that men had forgotten you. Today, God will remember you. He will send you help. Not only did Joseph's freedom come like a dream, several other good things happened to Joseph before that day was over. The God of Joseph is still alive and He has not changed. He will surprise you and me for good in Jesus Name.

David is another example; he woke up one day like any other day, and went on his normal business. Then about mid-afternoon he got a call to come over to the house. On getting home, he saw everybody standing including Jesse, his father. He must have wondered; 'what's going on here?' Then suddenly, someone started pouring oil upon his head and then proclaimed him the next king of Israel. To David it must have appeared like a dream!

In John 9:1-9, our Lord Jesus healed a man who had been born blind. The miracle was too real to be true. The people who knew him before could not recognize him again. It was a miracle like a dream.

In the great story we had been looking at (Psalm 126), the Bible called what God turned or restored "The Captivity of Zion". I believe the word "captivity" here refers among others, to the fortunes, and all the good things that the enemy had stolen or taken away - their <u>wealth, their treasures</u>, their <u>health</u>, their intellectuals (which was a great Brain drain to Israel), their glory, their entitlements, their rights and privileges. These may probably include many months or years of unpaid salaries, their retirement benefit sand pensions, etc among other things), and even their destinies!

This month, whatever good thing the enemy had stolen from you or denied you of, may God fully restore to you in Jesus Name. May your destiny be activated and accelerated in Jesus Name.

The Question arises as to why some divine interventions are described as "a miracle like a dream". I believe there are several reasons for it. For example, in many instances (if not most), the way God intervenes were always too real to be true!

There are times too when as men, we would have lost all hopes either because we have waited so long for a miracle and nothing had happened or because all our permutations had failed. In addition, 'Experts' may have told us there was no solution, then God stepped in and sprang a surprise, and like a dream, He made it happen! Today, a miracle like a dream will be your portion in Jesus Name. God will spring a surprise on our behalf in Jesus Name.

In Acts 12:5-12, Apostle Peter was in prison, awaiting execution. The Church mobilized prayers and Vigil.

Then God stepped in and delivered Peter supernaturally. The Bible said in Vs 9-11, that initially, Peter thought it was a dream. Let's read it:

> *"9 And he went out, and followed him; and wist not that it was true which was done by the angel; but thought he saw a vision. 10 When they were past the first and the second ward, they came unto the iron gate that leadeth unto the city; which opened to them of his own accord: and they went out, and passed on through one street; and forthwith the angel departed from him. 11 And when Peter was come to himself, he said, Now I know of a surety, that the Lord hath sent his angel, and hath delivered me out of the hand of Herod, and from all the expectation of the people of the Jews."*

It was not Peter alone who thought it was a dream, even those who were praying for him did not believe God could do it so fast or so soon!

This month, God will spring a positive surprise for you in Jesus Name.

One day, a little over five years ago, I just finished my morning devotion and Quiet Time when I had God impressing it strongly upon my heart that He was going to give us (RCCG Australia/Pacific Region) a Radio Station. About a year later, this became a reality. The day I was asked to come and pray to dedicate it (in Sydney), it was a miracle like a dream!

The miracle of a divine intervention that brought the children of Israel out of Babylon was not just like a dream, they said: *"Then was our mouth filled with laughter and our tongue with singing"*

I pray that this month, God will make you laugh. He will fill your mouth with laughter. People will come and dance with you. They will join you to sing <u>*ALLELUYAH*</u>!

Not only were the Israelites thrilled by the miracle God performed, even their enemies could not but acknowledge that this was God at work. Hear them:
> *"Then said they among the heathen, The LORD hath done great things for them."*

This means that those who had been mocking them - asking where was their God, were now the ones telling everybody: 'their case is different', 'We too must go and try their God!' (Please see also Dan 3:14-15, 26-30).

All who had been asking where is your God, all who had been mocking you, all who had been saying; we will see how you will do your own in this land - God will disappoint them. Very soon, they will come and celebrate with you.

Now, what those former mockers began to say is very instructive. They said: "*The Lord has done great things for them*". This was nothing but an advertisement for the Israelites, and of course, their God!

This is my hearty prayer for you. Very soon, in your work place, in your street, in your Suburb, God will give you divine advertisement in Jesus Name.

In conclusion, what are all these saying to us?
First, that you should know your God and learn to trust in Him (Psalm 37:25; I Peter 5:7)

Second, that you should not take Him for granted. Rather, you should fear and honour Him (Psalm 112:1-3).

I don't know what the enemy may have stolen from you whether physically or spiritually. Perhaps they did so in your dream, today, God will cause a full restoration in Jesus Name.

By God's grace, I have experienced some miracles like a dream on many occasions these include the supernatural gift of a car in 1991. Another was my appointment as a State Pastor in our Church/organization, all the way back in 1997. There is the miracle of the gift of a brand new car in a Mission field - in the far away 'ends of the earth' (Australia)!

You can be a candidate for a miracle like a dream.

The first step in experiencing a miracle like a dream is to have personal relationship with the God who has the power to perform miracles like a dream.

In Proverbs 28:13, the Bible says:
> *"He who covers his sins will not prosper, But whoever confesses and forsakes them will have mercy."*

In effect, what the Bible is saying here is that anyone who continues in his or her sins will remain in bondage and captivity! Dear reader, you now have a choice. I think it will be for your good to join in the following prayers:

- Father, anywhere and in any form I may have been in captivity - by birth, evil covenant, my own inordinate ambition, or due to the evil ones I associated with, please set me free this very day.

- Every blessing that I had lost or been denied of, Father, please restore to me today.

- From now on, let all who had been mocking me, begin to celebrate me.

- Father, the help that I need, please send to me right now.

- Father, give me a Miracle like a dream - in my body, soul, spirit, and in my finances.

- Father, like a dream, let my promotion come; let my Fiancé appear Like a dream, let that approval come forth. Like a dream, let my baby come.

May God answer all your prayers. May He fill your mouth with laughter and give you a new song - a song of Victory in Jesus Name.

May that letter or the call you have been expecting come very soon. May that interview and appointment you have been praying for become a testimony soon in Jesus Name.

May that long-awaited baby <u>boy</u> be on the way, and, may people join you very soon to shout a big Alleluia in the mighty Name of the Lord Jesus!

Acknowledgments

I thank God for inspiring this book that you have in your hand. I thank all the Brethren and friends who have continued to lift up our hands, and encouraged us in the work that God has called us to do, especially in this part of the world. They include John and Esther Adegboye, Femi and Faith Odumade, Abiodun and Temitope Doherty, Tunde and Kemi Fadahunsi, Wale and Bukky Omolokun, Kolapo and Kenny Adigun, Niyi and Olayemi Borire, Olaitan and Funmi Oyefeso, Stella and Akin Oyemade, Omowunmi and Isaac Adewunmi, Mary and Sam Olaniyan, and many more others. I wish to also specially thank Olusola Johnson of House of Israel Publishing Company, who did the cover design, as well as Mrs Funmi Agbi and Tunde Ajeyomi who took time to painstakingly go through the manuscript.

May the Lord continue to make all your affairs to run smoothly, and ensure you flourish in all you do in Jesus Name.

Finally, on the family front, I thank Jane - my wife of over thirty-five years, for all her love, prayers, and endurance. It shall never be in vain in Jesus Name.

Abraham Haastrup,
Melbourne, Australia.
August, 2021.

www.ingramcontent.com/pod-product-compliance
Lightning Source LLC
Chambersburg PA
CBHW070554010526
44118CB00012B/1312